Encounters
with Darkness

Encounters with Darkness
Copyright ©2001 by David Collinson

First published 2001

British Library Cataloguing in Publication Data.
A catalogue for this book is available
from the British Library.

ISBN 1 873796 95 1

Published by
Autumn House
Alma Park, Grantham,
Lincs., England, NG31 9SL.

10 9 8 7 6 5 4 3 2 1

Encounters
with Darkness

Christian victims of violence
tell their stories

by David Collinson

with additional material by
Sam Davis and Isobel Webster

About the Author

Revd David Collinson was born in Newcastle-upon-Tyne towards the end of World War II. He studied at the University of Durham and then trained for the ministry at Wesley House, Cambridge, under W. F. Flemington and Gordon Rupp. Ordained in Oldham in 1970, David has worked as a Methodist circuit minister ever since, serving in circuits all over Great Britain. He is married and has two daughters and a son, all now grown up.

My grateful thanks are due to

'Bill', 'M', Sam, Janice, John, 'Joanne', Mollie Waddell OBE, and Ken Mackintosh for writing or telling of their experiences; to Pastor Sam Davis and Isobel Webster for helping with the interviewing; to Helen Hopwood, my long-suffering secretary, for typing the manuscript; to David Marshall for licking it all into shape; and to my wife for her patience and encouragement. It is their book.

Thanks are also due to Janice Wiseman for permission to reproduce the chapter entitled 'Janice: Speaking about the unspeakable', which first appeared in her book *Cast Out, But Not Forsaken*, published by the Evangelical Press of Wales.

Editor: D. N. Marshall BA PhD

Readers: Professor John Walton, University of St Andrews; Pastor R. H. Surridge MA (Manchester); Nan Tucker FCP; Isobel Webster MA; Dr Andrea Luxton, Principal, Newbold College of Higher Education; Verna Anderson BA

Proof reader and copy editor: Anita Marshall

Cover design: David Bell

Foreword

by Professor John Walton PhD DSc FRSE
University of St Andrews, Scotland

This book will definitely be of interest to a wide cross-section of Christians, many of whom wrestle with the problem of why God allows the innocent to become victims of violence. Many Christians will be grateful for these insights into the lives and feelings of abused Christians. Particularly helpful are the dos and don'ts of sympathizing and relating to Christians who have suffered in these ways.

Some of the chapters are very inspiring and encouraging, such as Ken's story, where God's purpose is perhaps more clearly seen than in other cases. The policeman's story especially appealed to me as well, but all the chapters are interesting for one reason or another. Virtually all the individual authors come across as refreshingly and transparently honest, which gives their stories genuine impact and value, and the style of writing is of high quality.

Contents

Introduction

One December, some years ago, my wife and I had a rare evening off and went to a choral concert in Huddersfield Town Hall. We enjoyed the concert, which included Vaughan Williams' 'Fantasia on Christmas Carols', and left in serene mood, with its words ringing in our ears:

'God bless our generation who live both far and near,
And God bless you and send you a Happy New Year.'

Outside the hall, however, a couple of members of 'our generation' were fighting. A loutish character with tattoos on his arms and a drugged expression in his eyes was raining blows on the face of a punk rocker. Meanwhile, the punk rocker's girlfriend was screaming hysterically. My wife (who used to put the shot for her school!) said to me, 'We can't have this', and went over and interposed herself between the two lads.

'Leave him alone!' she snapped at the one with the tattoos. I joined in the attempt to break up the fight and, rather to my surprise, 'tattoos' backed away and slunk off.

I was glad that we had intervened, foolhardy though our intervention might have been; but it was a most unpleasant incident, one ingredient of the unpleasantness being that — out of all the mostly Christian concert-goers streaming out of the hall — no one paid any attention to the fracas except ourselves; the others were deliberately looking the other way.

Yet violence cannot be ignored, for it is, sadly, a growing feature of our society. In England and Wales there were 100,000 recorded crimes of violence against the person in 1981. By 1991 that figure had almost doubled to 190,000. In 1997 the figure had grown to 251,000. In Scotland we find the figures for these three years were 8,000, 16,000 and 15,000 respectively. As far as the crime of rape is concerned, the figures for England and Wales are 1981: 1,000; 1991: 4,000; 1997: 7,000, while in Scotland the figures (only available for 1991 and 1997) are 1,000 a year. Violent crime has apparently been generally increasing since the Second World War (*Social Trends* 29, pages 152, 153, London HMSO, 1999).

Faced with these facts, Christians above all people should be concerned and able to deal with violence both at its point of occurrence and during its aftermath. We cannot meaningfully pray 'God bless our generation' and then fail to back up our prayers with a willingness to be a part of God's means of blessing it; yet such involvement will inevitably lead at least some of us into encounters with violence, when it would be helpful to have some ideas on how to cope, and to help others to do so.

The experience recorded in the first chapter of this book caused me to think a great deal about how the spiritual resources of the Christian faith might be deployed to enable people to cope when facing violent incidents or their own psychological aftermath. I noticed, however, that very little appears to have been written about this subject for the layperson, especially from a Christian viewpoint. Therefore, when the Methodist Church, which I serve as a minister, gave me some sabbatical leave, I decided to put together a book of stories about Christians who had either experienced violence themselves, or been involved in helping those who had. This is the book you now hold.

Each story is told in the way its subject preferred, which explains why some are interviews; some are stories told in the first person; some in the third person. Some stories are specific about names, dates and places; others are deliberately vague about such facts, and names have been altered. This is because in those particular cases there may be a continuing fear of reprisals, or a risk of unwanted media interest. The subject matter is at times harrowing, but we have pulled few punches, not because we wanted to put together a kind of 'religious thriller', but because we wanted readers to gain from the stories a clear idea of what it is actually like to be a victim of violence. A number of contributors spoke of the failure of others to understand what they were going through; and one of the aims of this book is to remedy that lack of understanding.

Some readers may question the propriety of including a story about a rape and one about an indecent assault. I can only say that these things happen, and when they do it is important for the victim's friends to understand her experience and her reaction to it, and to be prepared to listen at length to her story, harrowing though it may be. To have refused to include such material would have been cowardly. The healing of such experiences may actually depend on opening up to others, and to be coy about them may actually compound women's difficulty in speaking about their feelings.

Our book's intention is to be helpful, both to victims of violence and those who are perplexed about how to help them. This is one reason why the book is short: it may have to be read at a time of great urgency and stress. However, it is our hope that when it is read it will offer helpful pointers as to how a Christian might cope when he or she 'encounters darkness'.

David

Climbing the Steps

I will begin with a pleasant memory. It is high summer in the Isle of Skye. Loch Scavaig is as calm as a millpond, and the Cuillin mountains which tower over it seem almost benign this day, despite their savage ridges and spires of rock. The boat that has brought my wife and me and other tourists to this spot chugs into a little jetty and ties up. Seals, cute and cuddly as long as you don't get downwind of them, are sunning themselves on a rocky islet. A beautiful white yatch is moored nearby, and its young crew are playing in a waterfall some way along the shore: you can hear their shouts and laughter a long way off, it's so quiet.

From the jetty we pick our way over rock and bog to the shores of another loch, Loch Coruisk. Normally, Coruisk is a wild and savage place, with more rock than vegetation round its shores, and cliffs at its head higher than any you'll find in the rest of Britain, but today even Coruisk seems to smile, and we stride happily over the whalebacks of gabbro by the loch shore. It's great to be back in the mountains, without a care in the world.

It is strange, though, how the Lord brought us to this place. One Thursday the previous November was a very different kind of day. Mind you, it began pleasantly enough. In the morning, I drove my car from our home on the outskirts of the town where I served as a Methodist minister, and parked it in the car park of my town-centre church. From there I walked to the station and took the train to another city a couple of hundred miles away, where I attended a day conference for ministers. Time passed, and I enjoyed the fellowship of a couple of other ministers on the return journey. But then they left the train at stops down the line, while I journeyed on to my destination alone. A strange depression, which I could not explain, seemed to envelop me as we approached home; and, as I set off from the station to walk back to my car in the church car park, a particularly dismal line of poetry by the World War I poet Wilfred Owen drifted into my mind: 'Slowly our souls drift home . . . .'

My route from station to church took me up a flight of seventy stone steps which emerge in the street where my church is located. The steps are straight and steep, have no landings on them, and used to be dark, too, until the local Council renovated them a few years ago, fitting them with a rail down the middle and lampposts at intervals. Even so, there is still something intimidating about them, especially in the misty darkness of a November evening.

As I approached the steps I saw that a couple of young men, in their late teens or early twenties, were standing a couple of steps from the bottom, blocking half of the stairway between the flanking stone wall and the central handrail. I thought nothing of this and set off up the other side; but as I passed the young men, one, who was much taller than the other, said to me, 'Got a fag, mate?'

'No, I'm sorry,' I said, and continued up the steps.

As I made my way up, I saw the tall chap run up his side of the steps and disappear round the corner at the top. Meanwhile, there was a group of young lads standing motionless on that side of the steps about halfway up. The police were later to interview these lads as witnesses, and discovered that they had been told by the shorter of the two young men to stand there and not to look round. Then, when the attack was over, the shorter young man, who had a look in his eyes as though he was on drugs, had waved them on. Their evidence also suggested that a bottle had been broken over my forehead.

However, I was not aware of this, because the last thing I remember was approaching the top of the steps and, oblivious of what was developing around me, seeing across the street to where my car stood in the church car park, and thinking, 'Ah, soon be home now.'

Then hell broke loose.

The next thing I knew, I was sprawled against the handrail, semi-conscious and seeing everything through a brown haze. Then I felt a heavy blow to my nose, either a kick or a head-butt, and blacked out again. A second or two later, I recovered consciousness again, only to find myself falling backward down the steps, and only managed to stop myself plummeting much further by grabbing hold of the central handrail.

'Oh no!' I called out. 'Oh my God!' But I felt no fear, only a sense of utter horror and dismay. I managed to crawl on all fours back to the top step, where the tall youth confronted me again. He aimed his boot at my face and I thought, 'Oh no, he's going to kick me again', but then something seemed to stop him, and instead he just said, 'Hand over your wallet or we'll do it again.'

I handed him my wallet. I have never had a problem with doing that, or thinking that I should have refused and fought back. I was by then in no state to fight back, and, in any case, the wallet, as it happened, had no money in it. They quickly disappeared. I later discovered that they had also got my briefcase, which contained a file of documents, a life of Stephen Hawking, a copy of *Surprised by the Voice of God* by Jack Deere, and a small Bible. I like to think that they kept them and read them, but that seems rather unlikely.

My first thought then was that I had to get home; so I staggered across to my car in the car park on the other side of the street, noticing on the way that I was dizzy and could not walk straight. And then I could not find my car keys, which was just as well, because I was in no condition to drive home. However, it happened that a music school which used our church premises was in progress at the time; so I staggered to the side door of the church and rang the bell. The door was opened by a young woman who must have got an awful shock to see me standing there with my clothes drenched with blood from my nose and a deep cut in my forehead. I explained briefly what had happened and then swept past her and along to the corridor to the gents' toilet to clean myself up, leaving a lot of bloodstains on the way. Two days later the bloodstains had to be dealt with before a coffee-morning could take place, and I think this gave the impression that not only had the minister been violated but the church had, too.

I ended up, of course, in Casualty, where they detained me overnight, as they always do when head injuries are involved. They also X-rayed my skull in case of fractures, but there was none, and then every hour through the night they woke me up and asked me what day it was, checking in case a blood clot was developing in my brain. I became annoyed at this procedure after some hours and nearly told the nurses to clear off. However, grace prevailed, and mercifully there was no blood clot either. Meanwhile, back home, my family hugged one another and cried and prayed for my recovery. I am blessed with a loving family who are all firm Christian believers. And I *felt* the power of their prayers and the prayers of others. Suffering as I was from concussion, I was unable to concentrate on anything for more than a very short period, so I was unable to pray for myself, but I was buoyed up by others' prayers. This was a wonderful discovery for me, for though I had often glibly told hospital patients, 'I imagine you've felt upheld by others' prayers,' I did not know for myself what this was like. Suddenly I did. It was luminously clear that God was with me, and I believe that this deepened my faith.

Physical recovery did not take very long. Besides the concussion, I had facial injuries, but, by God's mercy, no brain damage, no damage to my eyes, and no broken bones. This was remarkable, because the calculated viciousness of the attack and its location on the steps could all too easily have meant serious injuries, brain damage, loss of sight, even death. I did not, however, think it had 'just been luck'. I reckoned that I had been genuinely under God's protection. When I had set off that morning, I had prayed, as I always did, for 'journeying mercies' as the old saints used to call them. I therefore concluded that God must have had His reasons for allowing the attack, but had said to the forces of evil, 'Thus far, and no further.'

Before I left hospital, the doctor told me that my face

would look worse before it looked better, that I would need to take things easy for a week or two, and that a couple of days of depression were likely. For a few days I was indeed unrecognizable, as if I had gone a round with Mike Tyson, but that quickly cleared up: indeed the recovery seemed to escalate after a colleague came over to see me and pray with me. The only physical symptoms that lingered were dizziness and an inability to walk straight, which took some months to clear up, and a scar in the middle of my forehead which has remained to this day. The rest cleared up in a fortnight.

I wish I could write that this was all there was to it, that thereafter I went on with life and was able to put the unfortunate incident behind me. Sadly, this was not the case. Had I been merely the victim of an accident – had slipped and fallen down the stairs for example – I would have been able to move on quite quickly, but as I had experienced physical violence, the injuries were not the main problem: the psychological consequences were far more serious, albeit unpredictable.

Perhaps it is because so many of us comfortably-off middle-class people move through life with a false sense of security that, when it is brutally shattered, the shock is profound. There is thereafter a sense of deep insecurity and uncertainty. You now know that life can very suddenly turn very nasty. Not only that, you now know that people whom you liked, generally felt at ease with, and saw good in, can also very suddenly turn nasty. And that discovery in particular can be very shocking. You also feel as if not just your body but your personality has been violated. You have known love, and that love told you were special and valuable. Now something that happens tells you the opposite, that you are nothing; for even if the aggressor does not heap curses on you, denying your legitimacy and your morality – though he may well do so – his brutality will say this louder than words. To be a victim of violence is an experience that can shake one's personality to the foundations, at any rate for a while; and if one is a Vietnam War veteran or a former inmate of Auschwitz, the effects can last a lifetime.

So, I experienced psychological consequences, too. Funnily enough, *anger* was not one of them. My family felt considerable anger against the men who attacked me, but I felt none. They have yet to be caught, and I pray of course that they will be caught, because as long as they are at large many other people are at risk, but I do not want revenge. Does that mean that I have forgiven them? I'm not sure, but it has taken no mental effort to come to the point where I bear them no ill will. The anger just did not happen. However, other unpleasant reactions did occur. To begin with, I felt almost euphoric, as if the event put all smaller troubles into perspective, and even the most ill-tempered committee or council was going to be a doddle from then on, by comparison with what had happened to me. But suddenly, the depression predicted by the hospital doctor arrived and took up lodging in my mind, not just for a couple of days, but for some weeks.

The depression told me that this shattering experience was something I would never get over, that my life would never be the same again, that in fact I had discovered the truth about life, which was that life was fundamentally horrific for most people most of the time, and that if I had been thinking differently for fifty years it was only because I had been living in a fool's paradise. There was also a sense of horror: the way one might feel if one had just witnessed a dreadful accident; only there was no accident, just the feeling. In my mind, the town where we live became unpleasant and horrific and I particularly did not want to go near 'those steps'. This in turn, of course, made it difficult to go near my church, which was nearby, and for a while I hated going there and would only go to my own church if there were going to be a lot of people there. I experienced this depression intermittently for some weeks and then the tide, as it were, began to turn, and I think I can identify the moment when it did. I was standing in our kitchen at home, engaging in some small task or other, and the thought came to me (as it had done before), 'This is how life will be for you from now on: horrific.' I immediately found myself saying, 'Rubbish!', and from then on the depression, as such, began to clear up.

Other difficulties lingered, however. Some have cleared up wonderfully since, while others may still be around and likely to recur. I'm not sure. There were still some anxieties. For instance, a problem occurred around the Christmas following the incident. People in our church were in the habit of going carol singing. I got it into my head that this was really a rather dangerous thing to do and tried to persuade them to cancel the carol singing. They said they had had no problem with it in the past and didn't see that there was any such risk. In the event, off they went, but I could not bring myself to join them, which made me worried about looking a coward in front of my congregation. My state of mind was not improved by the fact that a couple of intruders – one tall and one short – attempted to enter the church premises during evening worship at about the same time. They were chased away by one of the congregation, but I was convinced that they were the same two men who had attacked me. I had not seen them, but I was sure it was they, and I felt humiliated by the fact that my anxiety was rather obvious.

However, this general jitteriness did pass, and the following Christmas I went out carol singing and enjoyed it, experiencing no fear whatsoever.

It is important to realize that some of these unpleasant psychological consequences do go with the passage of time. This may not be true of the severest traumas, such as those experienced by Vietnam veterans in the USA, but for many victims it *is* true. This thing that happened to you is not going to blight the rest of your life, necessarily, and you *can* move on. Sometimes, though, it helps if fears are faced up to. Like my fear of climbing those steps. I had a few days' holiday with the family after Christmas, and our plan was to leave our car in the church car park and walk to the station. Then on our return, one of us would walk back to the church – via the steps – pick up the car and bring it to the station to pick up the rest of us, plus baggage, and go home. I think on our outward journey my wife must have left me at the station first, and then parked the car, but I knew that on our return, one of us would have to climb the steps to get to the car. I thought I should volunteer; not be a wimp, but face it. I suppose I felt like Nehemiah in the Bible: 'Should such a man as I flee?' Rightly or wrongly, pride was involved. But the knowledge that I had the steps to face at the end of our long journey almost spoilt my holiday. In the event, when we got off the train on our return journey, my 15-year-old son said, 'Come on, Dad, I'll climb the steps with you,' and he did. Soon afterwards, I was able to make the ascent by myself, though it was to be some time before I found it easy to do so.

And then there was the exhaustion, which lingered for almost nine months. During that time, it seemed impossible for me to put in a full working day, and tasks were being left undone. I felt guilty about this, and the guilt became a kind of secondary problem. There was also a keyed-up, anxious feeling, a sort of vigilance and apprehensiveness which seemed to contribute to the exhaustion. The stress of all this lowered my resistance to infection and, as Easter approached, I was overcome by a whole series of illnesses and had to take to my bed. Unfortunately, in my line of work, it can be disastrous to fall ill, and one week I took to my bed just as a particularly busy weekend was approaching. We had a church weekend away, at a country house. Meantime, I had double-booked myself, and scheduled a 'circuit meeting' on the Saturday of that weekend as well. So I had to drive my family to the country house on the Saturday morning (we should have been there on the Friday evening, but I was too ill), then drive a hundred miles back to the church where our circuit meeting was to be held, then after the meeting drive back through the mountains to rejoin my people at the country house for the rest of the weekend.

I managed it all. I played worship tapes as I drove back through the dark and the rain from the circuit meeting to the church weekend. Praise is powerful. I am reminded of Paul and Silas sitting spreadeagled in the stocks in gaol at Philippi, having just been beaten with rods, and singing praises to God. I joined in and sang praises to God as I drove back, with the result that I arrived at the house full of energy. It was a fruitful weekend, at which one or two people took real steps forward in the Christian faith, and I stayed full of energy throughout. The contrast to the way I felt on Friday evening was unbelievable. But then, when we went home, I fell ill again. The experience of being 'under the weather', and yet being upheld by God, was very characteristic of this period of my life.

Victims of violence often speak of getting 'flashbacks', particularly vivid memories of the trauma they have experienced. I do not think I got flashbacks as such, but in times of severe stress some of the feelings of horror and dismay would return. I also noticed that I would experience occasional bad days when all my courage and confidence about anything at all would desert me. As long as ten months after the attack, I was still having such days, and vividly remember one of them.

I was an honorary university chaplain; so during 'Freshers' Week' I had to attend a reception for new students in the chaplaincy. I therefore duly turned up at the chaplaincy, walked into a room full of people, picked up a cup of coffee, and then thought to myself, 'I just can't face this.' After putting down the cup of coffee, I fled. Now this was not like me at all. During the 1984 miners' strike, when I was working in Yorkshire, I had gone out and visited picket lines at the local colliery in the early morning. By comparison with that, the student reception should have presented no difficulty, but it did. Such days have become fewer in frequency, but I have still not got the confidence that they will never return. I am actually in some ways a weaker, more vulnerable person now than I was in the days before the attack, but I live with that, because I remember Paul's words: 'When I am weak, I am strong.' In our weakness we hang upon God to a far greater extent than when we feel self-confident and strong. So it is most often the one who knows himself – or herself – to be weak who is used by God. It is often through pain and brokenness that He uses us most. When the healing we have prayed for, either for ourselves or for others, does not come, we perhaps need to remember that.

A victim of violence does need the help and understanding of others if he or she is to recover and move on. The Sunday after I was attacked, a carload of preachers from my church went out to take services in some of our small outlying chapels. There, they told the congregation what had happened to the Superintendent Minister, and asked for their prayers. As a result, I was deluged with cards expressing their concern, and assuring me that they would indeed pray for me. Later on, when I went out in person to visit those places, people flocked around me, wanting to know how I was. One lady said nothing to me, but just gave me a big hug. That meant a great deal. Many of the people from my own church were supportive as well. I did notice one curious fact, however. A significant number of people who must have known what had happened never mentioned it or inquired how I was. It may be that this was because they found it distressing to hear about, or because they did not want to dwell on something which made them feel that they, too, might be in danger. Perhaps they also thought that I might find it distressing to talk about it myself.

In fact, though, victims of violence do generally want to talk about the experience. Indeed, if they do not want to talk about it, it may be an unhealthy sign. I think I learnt this the hard way. You will probably have noticed that there was an element of pride in me, of being too proud to admit to being afraid, or unable to cope. This meant that I refused an offer of help from Victim Support soon after the incident, on the grounds that I did not want to think of myself as a 'victim'. I suppose, too, that I very much wanted to demonstrate God's power to heal, and thought that I would be letting Him down and letting down my flock if I could not do so. As a result, I was back in the pulpit a fortnight later, proclaiming how God had brought me through. This was not altogether a bad thing, but it did have the effect of making it difficult to talk about the incident or how I really felt about it. I also became aware that my story was pretty strong stuff; so I had to take care in choosing the ones in whom I should confide because not everyone could handle it.

When I did get the opportunity to talk about it – usually to our family doctor who was very understanding – I found some release, and the more gory detail I went into, the better I felt; but such opportunities were few and far between. I also kidded myself that I had recovered more quickly and more completely than I actually had, and would make such claims to others too. It has taken the experience of writing this book, in fact, to show me that I have not totally recovered – perhaps only 90% or so – and to teach me about the need to be honest, and not be ashamed of the continuing weakness I feel. I have learnt the hard way about the need for talk, and openness, and sharing.

The sharing has to be not only with others, but also with God. In fact, of course, other people's support is often God's way of supporting the victim. We have to be 'God with skin on' to one another. But it also helps very much if one has an ongoing, one-to-one relationship with God, and casts one's burdens upon Him. I sought to do that most of the time and, in among the anxiety and even the depression, there was still a sense of being upheld by God. For a lot of us Methodists, the hymns of Charles Wesley serve as a kind of prayer-book, and that is to some extent true of me as well. At this difficult time some verses of one of Wesley's hymns came to mean a lot, because they encapsulated my experience:

'Jesus, my all in all Thou art:
My rest in toil, my ease in pain,
The med'cine of my broken heart,
In war my peace, in loss my gain,

My smile beneath the tyrant's frown,
In shame my glory and my crown;
'In want my plentiful supply,
In weakness my almighty power,
In bond my perfect liberty,
My light in Satan's darkest hour,
In grief my joy unspeakable,
My life in death, my heaven in hell.'

Sharing the experience with God has also brought the conviction that God allowed the attack on me because He intended to bring good out of it. God's goodness far exceeded the evil wrought by my attackers. I have already mentioned some of the valuable things I have learnt from the experience. Another useful discovery has been the insight that the depression gave me into the world of the depressive. I now believe I can draw alongside victims of violence or sufferers of clinical depression with some understanding of how they feel. That's a great asset.

And then there is the 'wounded healer' principle. Some years ago I did some research which earned me the degree of Master of Theology. The research concerned the ministry of healing, and one of the things I discovered in the course of it was that people involved in such a ministry would often use the term 'wounded healer', indicating that you may be better equipped to heal broken bodies if your own body has been broken, and better equipped to heal broken hearts if your own heart has been broken. I concur with that principle, but I'm not quite able to explain why it should be so; and yet, the Bible does seem to bear it out. For example, in Isaiah 53, the prophet says, 'with his stripes we are healed.' Christians see this, of course, as referring to Jesus, the Saviour of the world, and you could argue that because of His uniqueness the same principle cannot apply to us. Other people might be healed by His stripes, but then He is the Son of God, and we are mere mortals. But the Bible also says that we are His body here on Earth, which means we share in His healing ministry, and the suffering that went into it. So I believe that God has been using the encounter to show me that the academic research, valuable as it was, would remain only at the level of theory unless I also became a healing person; and being wounded – and knowing ongoing weakness – was part of becoming such a person.

There have been all kinds of smaller blessings, too, like the writing of this book, and an award of £1,500 from the Criminal Injuries Compensation Board, on the strength of which my wife and I had a holiday in the Isle of Skye.

'M'
Targeted because she was a Christian

I had not met 'M' before I started work on this book, but she answered a letter I put in a magazine, saying she had a story to tell. A retired single teacher, living in a cottage in an idyllic village, she is a busy, vivacious person, full of joy in the Lord. The joy, however, has been hard won, as her story, written in her own words, will show.

It was a cold windless day, about halfway through December. Although business had been brisk at my Bible stall in a local market, the thought of a fire and a hot meal at home in my cottage was alluring. I packed up the car, pleased that the boxes were considerably lighter than in the morning, and drove the ten miles home. Home! a cottage consisting of five rooms side by side, two tiny cottages made into one at some time in the past. To dignify it by the term 'bungalow' was more pretentious than the humble little building warranted, but it was snug and 'home' in every sense, its quaintness calling forth admiration from friends. It stood by itself below a country lane, with two farms down the lane and one farm further up at the top of the hill. With fields in front where lambs disported themselves in spring, and fields behind with cows which lumbered up and down the lane at milking time – this was home!

The evening closed in, dusk bringing a light covering of snow. With a peat log on the fire giving off its own fragrance, and curtains drawn, the room gathered me into its peace and solitude. Bedtime, and I locked up and retired about 10.30.

Suddenly, I was awakened by the harsh sound of breaking glass. The greenhouse again? Panes had been shattered in a gale some months previously.

Jumping out of bed and putting on the light, I realized that there was no wind. Even as this jumble of thoughts flashed through my mind, the bedroom door burst open and a fellow rushed in – coat over his head, hands outstretched – shouting, 'Get down on the floor,' as he switched off the light. The shock was so great I screamed – not a pretty sound, a purely automatic reaction. As there was no one within screaming distance, I remember thinking, 'Save your breath for something more constructive!' I refused to lie on the floor, saying that the bed was more comfortable! And so it was – up to a point!

There was no avoiding the indecent assault which followed. I lay wondering what the next event would be.

'Father,' I prayed inwardly, 'am I going to be murdered now?'

'You are not coming Home yet,' He said.

'So, Father, what shall I say?'

A question came into my head, 'Have you ever done this to a woman before?'

'No,' was the fellow's answer.

'Then why pick on me?'

'Because you are a Christian.'

'Right,' I rejoined, 'and if you were a Christian you would not be behaving in this way. You are heading for a bad place unless you repent and believe in Jesus.'

With him still sprawled on top of me, I quoted John 3:16, 'For God so loved the world, that he gave his only-begotten Son, that whosoever believeth in him should not perish but have everlasting life.' I explained that 'perish' meant an eternity excluded from God's presence, and also quoted Revelation 3:20, 'Behold, I stand at the door, and knock: if any man hear my voice, and open the door, I will come in to him, and will sup with him.' I said he needed to open the door of his life and invite the Saviour in.

He then got up and left the bedroom but couldn't find the window which he had kicked in to make his entry. He called to me to let him out, which I did, putting him out at the back door, and watching him shamble off along the length of the cottage, snowlight giving me a dim sight of him, though I never saw his face.

The police came quickly at my phone call, and were absolutely marvellous, concerned and supportive. The cottage kitchen seemed full of large men for whom I made tea, but in my confusion I never thought to turn up the Rayburn, even though the night was bitter. I felt sorry for the poor policewoman, called out of a warm bed at 2am to come and join in.

My statement must surely have sounded somewhat different from those normally given to the police, as John 3:16 and Revelation 3:20 were written down in painstaking longhand. Indeed, there were a few surprised looks among my hearers.

The police doctor arrived; a physical examination was made; evidence was removed and I was left to gather my wits as best I might. My neighbours were questioned. Had they heard a car? Or heard anyone about? The wife of my nearest neighbour came to keep me company and help clear broken glass after the forensic people had gone. One policeman phoned a local builder, overriding his objection that he was too busy to reglaze my window immediately by official insistence that it should be done that morning. And it was!

An incident room was set up down the hill in the village and I was overwhelmed with loving and practical care from all and sundry. Offers of hospitality flowed in and I was glad to sleep away from the cottage for a few nights. Indeed, I wanted to 'purify' the bedroom, which I did by playing tapes of Christian music for a few hours.

'Will you go on living there?' I was asked several times.

'Of course,' I replied. 'It's my home and I'm not going to run away.'

(I may as well say here that I knew it was not going to be easy. Some nights I could not face it and begged a bed at one of the farms, but I was determined not to give in.)

As word spread, more and more kindnesses were showered upon me. A lovely little bunch of anemones arrived, their jewel-colours glowing, with a note hoping that their brightness would help to counteract dark memories. Another friend passed on a thought which I, in turn, have given to others – that memories are like clothes; they grow old and thin with time. My doctor said it might take five to seven years before I could come to terms with the experience. This was a real help, as it relieved me from feeling that I ought to be getting over it in a matter of days.

To my surprise, however, some of my Christian

friends seemed to question why this should have happened to me, one even going so far as to ask if I had lost my faith! There was only one reply to this: the words of Job 2:10, 'Shall we receive good at the hand of God, and shall we not receive evil?'

I had more difficulty in reconciling God's promises of protection with what had happened. My chief concern was that I was grieving our Lord because I could not at that time trust His Word. I knew how hurt I would be if anyone doubted a promise I had made, and my prayers were of apology for hurting my Lord because of my disbelief. When He said, for example, in Psalm 91:10, 'There shall no evil befall thee, neither shall any plague come nigh thy dwelling', what did He mean? I could quote many other verses on the same lines, all leaving me with the same question.

Eventually, I reasoned that my 'dwelling' was not the cottage, but the inner place where the real 'me' – my soul, if you like – dwelt, and this had been preserved from harm. Yes, evil had befallen me, but this had only bruised and hurt the outward part, my body, while the real 'dwelling' where my soul resided was untouched. I know this may seem far-fetched and even theologically rather odd, but it cleared up the problem for me, and, after all, I was the one who had been there!

So, why did it happen to me? I was doing an aggressive Christian outreach with Bible stalls and tract distribution; so the devil would not like it. And perhaps there was no other way in which my attacker might hear the Gospel, so was I trusted to cope, with our Lord's help? Only eternity may provide an answer to that.

My next market-day produced a question which I have treasured for its well-meaning absurdity and lack of perception. A customer asked, 'Was it you who was

upset by that gentleman the other night?' My answer
had to be 'Yes – a man, but hardly "gentle"!'

Time flowed by, the police enquiries producing no
results. Friends continued praying for me and one dear
friend told me she was praying that the fellow would
come forward and give himself up to the police. I had
never thought of that, but welcomed the idea as positive
and inspiring.

And then I began to discover how deeply fear had
taken hold of me. Later, when I tried to evaluate the
experience, I wrote:

Fear froze an icicle about my heart;
A sudden winter's chill encircled me;
Feeling and action, even thought itself
Suspended o'er a bottomless crevasse
Of blue-green terror . . .

I had for years been interested in, and occasionally
involved in, the Christian healing ministry. Now I was
helped by the laying-on of hands and prayer, but I still
had an overwhelming and embarrassing fear – I could
not bear to be in the company of any man, however
blameless he might be. One day I prayed in desperation
'Lord, this is ridiculous! Please deal with this now!'

At the time, a tent crusade was taking place locally
and I had been to some of the meetings, sitting by a
door to make a quick escape if necessary! At the
Communion service near the end of the crusade I crept
in and sat on the end seat of the back row. A couple
came in and the man sat next to me. I shrank more
deeply into my seat. Shortly, everyone began softly
singing the 'Holy, holy' from the Christian musical
'Come Together' which was popular at the time. This
always moved me deeply and the tears flowed. Very
gently, the man beside me put a hand on my shoulder

and all the fear of men drained completely away. It was almost a physical feeling of being emptied. My only regret is that I never explained the situation to that couple, as after the meeting they left rather quickly and I was still trying to regain some measure of calmness.

Two years passed, two years during which I prayed for my assailant each week on the day of the break-in and fasted with prayer on the actual anniversary of the attack.

Then other circumstances caused me to leave that lovely little cottage for a home some distance away.

One day, two detectives called at my house and asked me again about the night. They then told me that the man had come forward and admitted the offence, saying he had been 'in hell' ever since, because of what he had done to me that night. So that unusual prayer of my friend was the vital one! I was also complimented on the good description I had given of the fellow – remember that I had never seen his face!

'What next?' I asked the detectives. 'I don't want to press charges. He has himself to live with.'

'It doesn't rest with you,' they replied. 'Because of the gravity of the offence the case must go forward to the Director of Public Prosecutions, but we can say what you would prefer.'

'How long before I shall know?'

They shrugged. 'We can't say,' was their reply.

So, more urgent prayer. Though I had no fear of seeing the fellow again if the case came to court, I was worried because defence lawyers were apt to drag the woman through the mud and, though a 'fighter' spiritually, I still felt too drained to face a court case at the time. However, a few weeks later I was told that no action would be taken and the case was closed. The policeman who gave me this information said he

wished all their cases could be dealt with so smoothly;
so I suggested that prayer about investigations might
be beneficial.

I then plunged deeply into shock, shock delayed in its
intensity for two years! I had read that this was quite
usual when the case had been resolved, but nothing
could have prepared me for what it was like in reality.
Phobias? You name them; I had two of them.
Agoraphobia – even when I did get out of the house and
into my car and drove to the nearby town, I might be
unable to leave the car and would have to return home
without the shopping. On good days, with much prayer,
I might manage better. Claustrophobia – coming out of
church after a few minutes, shaking from head to foot.
. . . I cannot describe it. I once mentioned it to a
Christian friend. All I got was, 'God has not given you
the spirit of fear.' I exploded! 'Don't give me that,' I
raged, 'and don't quote Scripture out of context. Paul
wrote those words to Timothy to encourage him not to
be timid in his witness for the Lord.' I never told anyone again!

At that point, there was no one about who knew of
the healing ministry; so I laid hands on myself and
rebuked these fears in the name of Jesus. Things began
to improve. I went to a meeting with friends where a
chorus new to me was sung:

'Because He lives, I can face tomorrow;
because He lives, all fear is gone.'

All fear had not gone yet, but I could face tomorrow
– because He lives.

Four years after the event, God sent to me a clergy-
man who at the time of our first meeting knew nothing
of this story. He began to talk of the healing ministry of
the Church and his experience of it. To my surprise, I

found myself telling him what had happened to me, and how I was still feeling very insecure. 'We can do something about that,' he said, and laid hands on me with prayer. This was a very definite turning-point in my recovery, for which I give God thanks and praise.

So, looking back years later, I see this as my evaluation of the whole experience. Firstly, the obvious – that Christians are not exempt from physical or spiritual attack. Secondly, that it is in all these things that God can be glorified, and thirdly (and, to me, most importantly), He 'preserved my soul', my innermost being, the place of His dwelling.

I offer my story for the encouragement of others and to the greater glory of God.

Bill
Extra Time

My own experience of being mugged left me with a desire to know more about the effects of violence on its victims, to enable others to understand how they feel and help them to cope better with its aftermath. I also wanted to know what difference, if any, being a Christian made to the process of recovery or coming to terms with what had happened. So I began to seek out people who had been victims of violence and talk with them about their experiences.

I first of all went to see a man I know whom I will call Bill. The violence that Bill (not his real name) experienced occurred against the background of other significant things which happened to him at the same time, and, because the way he reacted to it cannot be understood without reference to that background, it needs to be sketched in. At the time it happened, Bill was in his late fifties, married and living in a town in the north-east of Scotland which made most of its living from fishing. He was not himself a fisherman (though his two grown-up sons were), but was well known and liked in the local Baptist church, of which he was a member, and in the community where he had lived virtually all his life and where he had a small business. Apart from a nasty car accident many years previously, his had been a successful and comparatively uneventful life – until, one November, Bill 'discovered who he was'.

Although he had lived most of his life in the north-east of Scotland, he had been born in Glasgow into a large working-class family. For some reason or other, the authorities had him fostered out when he was only a few weeks old, and he was brought up by an elderly widow in the place he came to regard as his home town. He had a birth certificate, and knew the names of his mother and father; and when he was a young lad he had visited Glasgow and inquired in the district where he was born if anyone knew the family. Nobody did, therefore Bill contented himself and got on with his life. Unknown to him, however, he had a sister in Glasgow who knew she had a long-lost younger brother somewhere. She and other members of her family had made enquiries for years, which were fruitless until that time when she finally established who her brother was and where he lived. In an atmosphere of enormous excitement, Bill was contacted and invited down to Glasgow. Thus it was that in November 1996 he travelled there to make contact for the very first time with his long-lost family.

For a couple of days, life was a whirlwind of activity and an emotional roller-coaster. Bill and his sister liked each other immediately, and she either invited him to her house, or took him to see what must have been scores of relatives. There was much laughter, and a few tears, as Bill made their acquaintance. By the evening of the second day, however, Bill and his sister were exhausted. She confessed that she had not slept for about a week and, as for Bill, his mind was full of new faces and facts and experiences which he needed time to digest, so he said to his sister, 'Look, we'll leave it at that tonight, and I'll see you tomorrow morning.'

He left his hotel and set off for a stroll. There were so many things on his mind that he was actually rather glad of some time to himself. In any case, although it was a November night, it was really quite warm. Bill's stroll took him a block or two to Argyle Street, one of Glasgow's main shopping streets, and he walked along it. Then he began to look for a phone box where he might telephone for a taxi, and he did come upon a line of three of them, but they were besieged by a group of scruffy young men, lounging around drinking. Bill decided to give these a miss and see if he could find another call box, so he walked on.

It was about then that Bill caught sight of a young girl on the other side of the street. She would have been about twelve years of age, and he noticed her because it was late, and he could have understood her being out late if she had been hanging around with some other youngsters of her own age, but she was standing alone, motionless, as if waiting for something. He walked on for a short while, then decided he was unlikely to find another phone box that way and it would be better to make his way to the Central Station and take a taxi from there. So he turned on his heels and set off back. In a short while, however, he came across the girl again. She appeared to have moved on a few yards, but was still standing alone. A little further along, Bill came to some traffic lights. By the traffic lights, the buildings did not meet at the corner, and the space between them had been planted with shrubs.

It was then that it all happened. In an instant someone came at him from behind, put an enormously powerful arm around him, and with the other hand held at his throat a huge knife, fully eight inches long with a serrated blade. Meanwhile, another man came at him from the front and grabbed him by the lapels, whereupon they both dragged him into the shrubbery. Bill, meanwhile, tried desperately to hold the knife away from his throat.

The man in front began to rant and scream obscenely at him: 'Give me your money! Give me your so-and-so money!'

Half of Bill's mind was in turmoil, but the other half of his mind seemed to drift into a detached, very alert mode, with everything slowed down, surreal. 'I'm dead,' he thought, and yet he was able to note the details of what was going on: he noted that although he could feel his assailants' breath on his face, there was no smell of alcohol, and he concluded that the motive for the crime was drug addiction.

There was no question of retaliation, he thought. As a younger man, he had been quite athletic and well able to defend himself, but he had the sense to know that a man approaching sixty had little chance of effectively defending himself against two very strong, very desperate young men. He was also, as it happened, a Justice of the Peace, and he and his fellow-magistrates had often had lectures from police, solicitors and other professional people, about the ways of the criminal fraternity. One such talk had been about how to conduct oneself if attacked. The idea was not to take the aggressor head-on and try to meet violence with violence, but rather to try to keep in control of yourself, to keep in control of the situation. It was necessary, they said, to keep everyone calmed down, let the attackers have what they wanted as long as it wasn't your life, and get them to leave. Effectively, it meant buying yourself out of the situation.

So that was what Bill did. 'Okay, guys,' he said, 'just wait a minute. Yes, keep calm; I'll help you. I'll give you my wallet. It's okay, guys, just keep calm.'

This seemed to have no effect on the man in front, who continued roaring and shouting, and then he produced a knife, saying that if Bill didn't give him everything he'd got he would stab him to death. 'I've already told you,' said Bill, 'just let me be and I'll give you what you want. Just shift your arm a bit.' He did loosen his arms a little, and Bill proceeded to go through his pockets, helped out by the noisy one who tugged brutally at his zip, his clothing and all his pockets until all his valuables had been removed.

'Okay, come on; let's go!' said the man behind. But the one in front had not finished. 'I want that ring off your finger,' he said.

Bill had got that ring when he was engaged, and it had never been off his finger in about thirty-five years. Worn and scratched, it nevertheless had great sentimental value.

'Give me your ring,' screamed the guy in front.

'Look, guys,' said Bill, 'I've given you everything you want, but please, please leave me with the ring. It's not worth much.'

But the guy in front began pulling at his fingers to remove the ring. It wouldn't budge. 'Okay, no problem,' he said, brandishing his knife, 'I'll take off his so-and-so finger.' But Bill wet his finger with saliva, and, by dint of using his teeth and drawing blood, he got the ring off. Then they forced him to the ground and held him there. 'Now, you don't move from here for ten minutes. If you move at all, we're going to come back and we're going to stab you to death. You know what I'm saying? If you move, someone's watching you.'

There was indeed someone watching him. It was the girl. She was their accomplice.

As Bill lay there in the shrubbery, he prayed. From a child, he had always been conscious of God, and that consciousness had grown with the years. Even when he was being brutally handled in the thicket, he had already been praying, 'If I come out of this, it's Your will, O Lord. It's You who is going to get me through this. Help me, O Lord, to keep my head, to keep calm, to keep collected and be in control of the situation. Other things don't matter. My life does.' But then unbelief came and did battle with belief and he thought: 'Here's me; left Glasgow as a child; I come back as a man in his late fifties and I've got to go home in a coffin.' The ten minutes passed, however, and Bill realized that the trio were not coming back. He had a cut in his ring finger, but otherwise there was not a scratch on him. 'Thank you, Lord,' he prayed. 'I'm still alive.'

Then he staggered to his feet. He was rather disorientated, and felt a need to tell someone what had happened; so when a little red Ford Fiesta pulled up at the adjacent traffic lights, he looked in at the window of the car, but the elderly lady driver shot him a look of sheer terror and locked all her doors from the inside, presumably under the impression that he was drunk. So he trudged on, dazed, towards the city centre. After a little time, he passed a McDonald's burger bar, with a man selling papers on the pavement outside, and he approached him. 'I've been attacked,' he said. 'I've been mugged. Can you get a policeman for me?' The newspaper vendor just looked at him.

'You all right, son?'

'Yeah. I'm okay.'

'You just go along here, and there's a police station

round the corner. Want me to come wi' ye? Are you going to make it?'

'I'm okay. I'll make it.'

The sergeant on duty at the police station also thought Bill was drunk. 'I've just been mugged,' Bill explained. The sergeant, of course, did not turn a hair. This was all in the line of duty to him; but he was kindly, and he offered Bill a glass of water.

'Now,' he said, 'we'd better get some details.'

'Can I phone my wife first?' Bill asked, and was allowed to do so.

Bill's wife is a very level-headed woman, and though the news over the phone must have been distressing to her, she told him that she would phone one of his new-found nephews, tell him what had happened and ask him to come out and see his Uncle Bill. He surely would come out, she said, because it was an emergency.

The sergeant and a colleague then began to take details. When he told them about the girl they asked him, 'Did she have fair hair?'

'Yes, she did.'

The two policemen looked at each other knowingly. Similar crimes had happened before, it appeared. Then: 'How much money did they get off you?'

'About £400.'

'That's probably what saved you from getting a good knifing, just the fact that you had money. That's what they're after. With plenty of money, especially if it's treasury notes, off they go and it's something to spend, on drugs probably. They've no more interest in you after that.'

Two plain-clothed officers appeared. It seemed to Bill that Starsky and Hutch had nothing on these two. They were tough, serious, totally street-wise, good at their job, and perhaps a little arrogant. They showed Bill what seemed liked hundreds of 'mug-shots', and then took him out in their car for a while, wanting him to show them where and how it happened, even having him take them into the shrubbery. Then, their work done for the time, they took him back to the station.

Eventually, the young men were to be apprehended and brought before the court, but the verdict was that infuriating Scottish category, 'Not Proven'. However, as they left court they were arrested immediately on other charges.

All this, of course, was some time in the future. At his new-found nephew's home on the outskirts of Glasgow, Bill talked far into the night, going over and over again all the details, and how he felt about it. He was very much aware at this stage of a need to talk and talk, and talking must have made a major contribution to his healing.

Then in the small hours, Bill was driven back to his hotel. He was surprised to discover that he slept very well, and woke in the morning glad to be alive and warm and safe. He does not hesitate to use the Christian phrase 'born again' about his experience. When, later that morning, more of his new-found extended family began to arrive, having been informed of the incident by Bill's wife, they saw that his bills were paid and put him on the train back home.

By that time the need for talk and human contact had receded. Bill had often found in the past that while travelling on the train up north he would meet friends and acquaintances from back home, but on this occasion there was no one on the train that he knew, and he was glad, because he had entered a new stage where he withdrew into himself, cutting himself off from other people and just being calm and still. Yet he was glad to be going home, to family, friends, the familiar, his own fireside. On arrival home, however, he began to shiver and tremble violently, and this did not abate, even though his wife turned up all the heating. During the night he woke up from time to time, trembling and sweating. He was in deep shock. But when, next day, he went and saw his brother-in-law, a wise and good Christian man, and talked for hours, he felt a kind of release at last.

To all intents and purposes, Bill appears to have recovered fully from his ordeal. He revels in the contacts with his new-found family, and when his sister, sadly, died a year or two later, he spoke briefly at her funeral. For a while, he could not bear the thought of anything sticking into his throat, and went about wearing a roll-necked collar. Flashbacks – vivid relivings of the event – did occur, one of them triggered by his witnessing a similar event acted out in a television thriller. But he is his old self, happy and vigorous and busy about various community projects.

His recovery strikes me, in many ways, as a textbook example of effective recovery from violent trauma. He understood the need to talk out the shock and hurt, and those around him appeared to have understood this need, too. He considers also that the event was overshadowed by the many new, good and exciting things that were happening in his life at that time, and have continued to happen; the darkness was swallowed up in the light. Then again, the hate and brutality shown him was more than counterbalanced by the love shown him by his own families, old and new.

All these things are forms of God's presence. Moreover, the event was not meaningless and valueless. I sometimes wonder if the Post-Traumatic Stress Disorder experienced by veterans of the Vietnam war was made much worse because the men did not return home to open-armed appreciation and glory: what they had been through was not deemed meaningful and valuable. Bill, however, found meaning and value in his trauma. He felt that it gave him an empathy and an insight, greater than he had known before, into the pain and agony of others. He also had an overwhelming sense of being spared by God because God had more for him to do. He claims he has been given extra time.

Sam
Can I help you, officer?

Sometimes violence is racial in origin, and sometimes violence is actually perpetrated by the forces of law and order. These two types of violence are combined in the ugly incident in which Sam and his friends were involved. The incident took place in 1988 and, there-fore, may or may not have represented part of the aftermath of the racial disturbances at the Broadwater Farm Estate.

It had been an excellent week-long spiritual retreat. Sam, Trevor, and Winston, three black young men, had been there. The camaraderie and fellowship had been excellent.

Barry C. Black, one of the finest black American preachers and an American Navy chaplain, had been the youth speaker. Black is a Rear Admiral and the US Navy's highest ranking chaplain.

Sam admits that his spiritual life when these events took place was not as it is now. While he enjoyed the spirit of the meetings, he was primarily there to meet his friends and have a good time. The week over, the three friends took their time packing up, exchanging telephone numbers and addresses with new friends, and then headed back to London travelling in convoy with some other friends.

They had just reached Tottenham, where one of their number was going to be dropped off, when they noticed a police car following them. The presence of a police car always has the effect of reducing speed and enhancing the quality of driving. It followed them for some time. They hoped it would turn off before too long. However, the three friends experienced that sinking feeling as the lights from the car flashed, indicating that they should pull over. Uppermost in their mind was the question, 'What have we done wrong now?'

The three guys got out of the car. Their driver spoke to the approaching officer whose partner had remained in the police car: 'Can I help you, officer?' They were surprised at the aggressive and hostile manner of the policeman: 'What are you doing around here? Is this your car? We noticed that one of you dropped rubbish out of the window.' The fellas volunteered to pick up the rubbish so that they could be on their way.

The rubbish that had been dropped was retrieved. The young men said, 'OK, officer, we've picked up the rubbish. Can we go now?' By then the policeman had become abusive, and was using foul language.

'Look, we've done nothing wrong. Can we go now?'

Sam noticed that the officer who had stayed behind was standing a little way off talking on his radio. They had, by this time, been in conversation with the officer for about two minutes when there were sirens and flashing blue lights. Two police vans and a Metro screeched up and policemen jumped out.

'We were bemused because we were thinking, "No, they can't be for us, we ain't done nothing," ' Sam says. 'I was grabbed around the neck, thrown to the ground, and at the same time they were using the most profane language I had ever heard.

'"You bleep, bleep, jungle bunny, you bleep, bleep, nig nog, you bleep, bleep baboon." I was on the ground with a knee in my back, my hands yanked behind, while I was handcuffed. My friends, Trevor and Winston, got the same treatment. In fact I believe Trevor got worse. The officers were f...ing and blinding. At no stage was there, "We're arresting you for . . ." or, "You have the right to remain silent, but whatever you say may be taken in evidence." Nothing.

'Before we were bundled into the van I shouted to our other friends who had stopped when we were stopped: "Follow the van!" Again there was just the constant, foul-mouthed racial abuse. The three of us were surrounded in the van, the handcuffs tearing into our wrists, and our clothes a total mess. At this time we decided to pray. It was the only thing we could do. I actually thought they were abducting us to beat us up at the police station or, even worse, to kill us.'

It was surprising to Sam that something as outrageous as this could be happening on a main road in London. It was early evening. It wasn't dark. Indeed, it was in the full glare of the public – and yet nobody seemed to care.

The young men were taken to the Tottenham police station which, as Sam was to learn later, was at that time notorious for its racism. However, the lads were not left to fend for themselves. As Sam describes it, providential help came from an unexpected source.

'We were in the van for a few minutes before we drove off. While we were there a man came up to the van. I recognized him as Bernie Grant MP. He asked the officers what was going on. Man, was I glad to see him! But they were thoroughly disrespectful and basically told him where to go. I was amazed! Here was an MP who had responsibility for helping run the country – and they told him where to go!'

The three friends were taken to the police station and charged with obstruction. Their immediate response was, 'Obstruction of what?' But then self-preservation took over. The most important thing now was to get out of the police station alive and in one piece.

'Here were people with a level of hostility so high that wisdom dictated that we do as little as possible to inflame what was already a very volatile situation.'

Fortunately for the young men, their other friends followed them to the police station, as did Bernie Grant MP. His intervention alone took the situation to another level. As Sam said, 'This was no accident; God put him there for a reason.'

The following day Mr Grant raised the matter in Parliament and within two days the young men were being interviewed by the BBC and ITV. This was no longer a local matter but one that had taken on national significance.

Bernie Grant was also instrumental in getting lawyers who specialized in civil rights cases. The incident had taken place in October and a court case was scheduled for December. Again Sam says, 'Within two weeks we saw the police case against us. It was almost as bad as the incident itself. It was a catalogue of fabrication and lies. . . . They had just sat down and said, "OK, how can we make this stick?"

'They changed every detail of the story. They said that when they had looked into our car they had smelt a "sweet smell like marijuana". They also said that they had seen a video recorder in our car that had made them think we were stealing. We were accused of making masturbating signals, and using foul and abusive language at them.' Of course, the officers painted themselves in the best possible light. They said that they had only lightly restrained the lads while coming under a constant barrage of swear words.

In fact the officers, in fabricating their evidence, had inadvertently played into the hands of their victims. They had failed to realize that, as Christian young men, these guys neither smoked, drank, nor used foul or abusive language. And there was a whole church community willing to testify to that fact!

At £360 an hour the lawyers did not come cheap. Sam's mother backed him 100% without any hesitation. So did the family and church friends of the other two lads. The fact that the officers had been so 'over the top' with their fabrication made it easy for the defence team to prepare their case.

On the day of the trial at Archway Magistrates' Court the families of the young men were present, and their character witnesses and church friends were out in force. They were, in fact, well supported. The police went first, giving their evidence. Sam says, 'It was embarrassing. Our barrister was able to expose their lies to the extent that they just stood there looking at the judge and saying, in effect, "I'm sticking to my story, that's all I can say, I'm sticking to my story." I just felt sorry for them.'

At the end of the first day in court, without the friends being called to give their testimony, the chief magistrate declared, 'We have decided of our own volition that there is no case to answer.' Sam says, 'I had never been to court before and at the time I didn't know what he meant. I looked around and asked, "What do we do now?" Someone said, "That's it. It's over." '

'That's it?' Sam just kept asking. He couldn't believe it. Someone said, 'That's it. You're free to go.' Says Sam: 'We just looked up to heaven and gave God thanks. I felt so elated, I'm pretty sure I was in tears at the time.'

God rewarded the faithfulness of these young men. Sam was working in a Job Centre at the time and was fully aware of the implications of a criminal record for his employment prospects.

I asked Sam if he could ever trust the police. 'For about two years after that incident I was extremely nervous every time I saw a policeman. I felt that I was a marked man and that they were going to get me. They knew where I lived, where I worked, everything about me. . . . But God gave me the victory over that fear. I was in Tooting Broadway two years after the event when I saw a policeman giving a black lad a hard time. I stood there and told him that I was watching and would be willing to act as a witness. From that day on my fear of the police left me.'

Sam believes that God has given him the ability to forgive the police for the abuse perpetrated against him and his friends that day.

'There were two officers especially that I struggled with feelings of anger against,' he says. 'They showed no remorse or regret – just total contempt for us and the court. Their attitude was, "They've done it and that's it." That was difficult to live with. Sometimes I feel that God takes control and I'm in His hands. Therefore, I should not harbour malice against any man. Other times it's not anger, it's pain – because my life was threatened. I hadn't done anything wrong. But then I'm reminded of what Jesus went through for me and the abuse that He took even though He had done nothing wrong, and He never said a mumbling word. In a sense I was given a taste of what Jesus went through, and if that can help me trust Him more and believe in Him more then it had a positive purpose.'

Two years after the incident Sam and his friends accepted a generous out-of-court settlement from the police for their wrongful arrest and malicious prosecution, although the police refused to admit liability.

God's grace has brought Sam to the point where he is today. He continues to witness for his faith through singing in the London Adventist Chorale – winners of the 1994 Sainsbury's Choir of the Year competition. He has been a youth leader and is currently a church elder. The wounds have been healed and the police forgiven but they can never be fully trusted. To do so would be to deny the event and the stories of those who have died in police custody because of their race. God continues to give the grace not to hate but to love.

John

A policeman's lot

It intrigued me – and has continued to intrigue me – that while some people can be shattered by a solitary experience of violence, others seem to be able to cope with repeated experiences of violence without any serious psychological damage – police constables, for example. With this in mind, I talked one day over coffee with my friend John.

John is a tall, distinguished-looking man who nowadays looks after a city-centre parish as a minister of the Church of Scotland, a job which he carries out with a rare mixture of showmanship, love and compassion. Although he is now in his mid-fifties, he has not been a minister for very long, having spent most of his life in the police force. I knew from what he had already told me that his work as a bobby had brought him into contact with some traumatic events. He had been present at the aftermath of a huge gas explosion at a place called Clarkston Toll when a shopping mall collapsed, killing dozens of people; and, on another occasion, had helped to rescue from a collapsed building a gravely-injured crane-driver who said as he died, 'Tell ma wife and weans I love them.' However, I wanted to know more specifically about acts of violence per se, and how he had coped with them at the time and afterwards.

First he gave me some background information. He started as a policeman in 1961 in a little Scottish burgh called Johnstone, just outside Paisley. Later, he was at Greenock, Port Glasgow and Gourock, before spending eighteen months in the more metropolitan atmosphere of Manchester. Returning from Manchester for family reasons, he resumed serving as a constable on the south bank of the Clyde. Over the years, the small police forces in which he served amalgamated with one another until, in the mid-1970s, they became part of Strathclyde Constabulary, a force with 8,500 officers.

I wanted to know if John had been a Christian throughout that time.

He sighed. 'I was a church member and went to the occasional communion service, but could only be described as a number on the communion roll. Then, I was working more with community groups and I joined a body called the CPA – Christian Police Association – which is a body of Christian policemen throughout the world. I was amazed at the number of policemen who were committed Christians. From then on things really started to happen in my Christian life, and I began to see things in a totally different way, not only in my own life but in my police work as well.'

The communities in which this young constable with the deepening spiritual awareness and widening spiritual concern worked were not genteel.

'I worked in Port Glasgow, for example, a shipyard area where a man was a man, and I saw all sorts of things: Friday-and-Saturday-night violence, fightings, stabbings, rapes, murders even. It was an accepted way of life. The violence went along with the type of lifestyle many had, which involved hard drinking, gambling, and – to a lesser extent in those days – drugs. On a Friday and Saturday night you knew what was going to happen and you weren't surprised by what happened. You just dealt with it accordingly.'

I got a sense from him that violence was less traumatic for a policeman than it would be for a 'civilian' like myself, who encountered it in a totally unexpected and uncontrolled way, because the policeman knew what to expect, was ready for it and was to a degree in control of the situation.

There were, of course, many occasions when John himself was on the receiving end of the violence:

'The first occasion when I was on the receiving end,' he said, 'was when I – foolishly – went by myself to investigate a disturbance in a public house. There were three men fighting with one another, and I tried to separate them. Although they'd actually been fighting with one another, the policeman was perceived as the common enemy and the three of them turned on me and I got a hiding. I remembered that we'd been told in our training at police college to take up the "foetal position" if attacked; so I did, and was conscious of blows being rained on my head and on my backside, while I tried to protect my stomach and face.

'The police van arrived almost in a couple of seconds, but it seemed an eternity, with all the blows being rained on me. I didn't realize how extensive it had been till the next day when all the bruises began to show, and I was in a lot of pain, and had to go to the hospital to be looked over. My uniform was in tatters; and it was later produced at the court case which led to the three men being imprisoned for aggravated police assault.

'Then, about 1979 – I'm not sure of the actual date

– I was stabbed in a bus shelter. Again, it was crowds spilling out of a pub; they'd been fighting, and I came upon it and they broke up, and one man lunged at me with what I thought was his fist, but I didn't realize that it was a knife. What prevented the stabbing from being more serious was the fact that I was wearing one of the heavy serge greatcoats which policemen wore in those days. The knife had penetrated the coat, through the uniform into my stomach only an inch or so, but enough to cause quite a serious injury. I was not aware of it; I arrested the man and took him up and booked him, charged him in the police cell; and it was only then that I became aware of the fact my clothes were soaking wet, and I saw the dark stain of blood and realized I'd been stabbed. It was difficult to prove, because I hadn't seen a weapon at the time, but he was charged with aggravated police assault, and he received a prison sentence for that. It's one of those occupations where you have to accept that if you go into a violent situation you can expect the violence to be directed towards you.'

I pointed out to John that the people who have contributed to this book all speak of the psychological after-effects of violence. 'Surely,' I said, 'it must have psychological effects on policemen as well. Have you found that?'

'I can't honestly say,' he replied, 'that there was any psychological effect, inasmuch as I didn't become withdrawn; and I didn't become depressed. I didn't go into myself or not want to carry on being a policeman. That never happened. What the violence towards me created was anger towards the person who had perpetrated the violence. There was a "revenge syndrome": I wanted to exact a suitable punishment for him from the courts for what he had done to me, and I think, at that particular time, that was how I got it out of myself.'

Was there, I wondered, a culture of 'machismo' in the police force, and did that have an effect on how policemen coped with violence? John did not feel that there was as much machismo as there once was.

'There used to be. Policewomen, for example, were few and far between. Any policewomen you had were kept indoors and dealt with minor child offences or female-related crimes. We called out a policewoman to do searches or to lock up a female prisoner. They were more or less kept in the office, typing, doing reports and similar things. So, yes, in the early days it was very much seen as a macho sort of job. That has changed, and for the better, as far as I am concerned, because policemen are servants of the public, and I don't think they should be seen as macho men but as part of the community. In the city where I work a lot of the policemen I know these days are working with the community, and the image they're trying to put across is, "Come to us; we're not bully-men. We want the children to speak to us; we want mothers with children to come up and chat to us. We want people to stop and talk to us. We don't want to be seen as something apart." So, I think it's an image the police themselves are trying to eradicate.'

He did, however, consider that the machismo actually helped the police to cope with violence. 'It made it easier to cope with because it was expected of you. The force did not give you any sympathy. If you got into a fight and came out second best, they just told you either that you shouldn't have got into a fight, or that you should have fought a lot harder. And you always remembered that, and, if you went into a fight and came out second best, in many cases you didn't take it any further – there was the shame of not winning over.'

'John,' I said, 'what interests me about what you're

saying is that when a person who is not accustomed to violence – who hasn't taken it as part of his job – encounters violence in the middle of what is a fairly comfortable life, (from what I'm discovering) he, or she, finds it shattering; and yet, here you are, and you've experienced assault at a similar level of seriousness a number of times, and it has not had that shattering effect. Is it the anger that has made the difference?'

'I don't think so,' he replied. 'I think it's possibly the initial training policemen go through. At training college we were taught how to deal with certain situations. Many times I've made use of what I was taught, and I've found it effective. For example, you could be in a situation where the man you've got to arrest is twice the size of you. The natural reaction would be to back off; but there's a way of controlling a person, of speaking to him, and if you follow the procedures – and these procedures have been built on over the years by experienced policemen – they usually work.

'Ninety-nine times out of a hundred you can talk people out of a violent act. They have committed, perhaps, a minor offence which is going to see them fined £20, £25, or something like that. The moment they hit a police officer in uniform it carries the minimum of at least two years in prison. Aggravated assault carries up to fourteen years, or even life. So you try to relate to them the error of their ways.

'Now look,' you say, 'if you hit me, you're going to get five years instead of being fined £25.' Talking to people, and giving them time, as it were, to count to ten, helps. There are also holding procedures. You learn how to hold a man to prevent his being violent. You can incapacitate a man with one hand so that he can't move, and all you're doing is holding his thumb in a particular way. Nobody, not even the strongest man on this planet, can get out of that hold. Nine times out of ten that worked for me personally.'

'So, is there any advice you would give to anyone facing a violent act, or the possibility of a violent act? Is there something he or she ought to remember?'

'The first thing to remember is: try to talk them out of it. But if you see they're still intent on committing the violent act, then you must accept the fact that you're going to be attacked, and, as I said, the foetal position, curled up on the ground, is the safest position if you get knocked to the ground. Roll yourself up into a ball, protect your face, your stomach and your chest, because these are where the vital organs are located, and any blows that are rained on you are rained on the less vulnerable parts. That's the only advice I can give to anyone. The natural human reaction is to retaliate, but that's the wrong thing to do, especially if there are more than two or three of them. You can deal with one; sometimes you can deal with two, but when there are three, even though they're a lot smaller than you, the odds are against you and it's better to sort of take it. That would be my advice.'

Then I thought it was time to change the subject, and I asked John what difference his moving from being a nominal Christian to being a committed one had made to the job.

'Well,' he said, 'I found my attitudes towards people were actually changing. It became well known that I was a very active Christian, and the first things I noticed were among my own colleagues. If they swore or took the Lord's name in vain, they would apologize if I was there. They might have been saying something behind my back, but that didn't concern me! What I found most of all was that in myself I was becoming more tolerant towards people and this sort of "revenge"

attitude left me. I didn't want to retaliate in that way
any more; I wanted to help people. I started to ask
myself, "Why do people want to do that? Why do they
want to attack me? What is their reason for it? Is it
authority they're hitting out against? Is it the background from which they come?" '

Christians not only have particular attitudes towards
others, but they often speak of experiencing God's
protection as they face life's risks. I wanted to know if
this had been John's experience. Surprisingly, it had not
been the case, not at the time. And yet, he did have a
powerful awareness of God's guiding hand, preparing
him for something.

'Looking back over my life,' he said, 'I can see very
much my police work, my training and progression
through the police force, as preparation. I used to ask
myself, "Where am I going? Where will I be in five years
or ten years? Why am I never promoted into the
ranks?" And the reason probably was that if I had been
promoted into the ranks, I would have gone through
the ranks, and never had the opportunity of going to
university and becoming a minister. I think that's my
excuse for not climbing the promotional ladder; because
one of the young men I started with is now a Chief
Constable, but most of them are retired, doing security
jobs and those sorts of things. That wouldn't have suited me. I think it was a sort of training.

'I'm always reminded of Jeremiah chapter eighteen –
the story of the potter's wheel and how there was this
lump of clay in the hands of the potter, which was
spoiled and thrown away, but which was then taken up
again and remoulded and made into another vessel. I
feel very much as though I'm that piece of clay that was
discarded and remoulded by the Maker's hands, to do
something for Him rather than for myself. There are no

two ways about it, David. I've now been ten years in my present parish, and I've been in the ministry for fifteen; and when I think of some of the situations I've had to deal with, I realize that people who did not have my sort of background and training would not have been able to cope. It's helped me to cope with multiple deaths, depression, suicide, and so on.'

I concluded by putting to him a question which may have been theoretical, but which seemed, and still seems to me, to be very important. 'Can we expect the God who loves us to protect us? And if we can, why do so many people, Christians included, experience violence?' His answer was unhesitating.

'Well, my angle on that, is that Christ suffered on the Cross for us, and if we are to relate to Christ, we have to suffer. If we want to be followers of Christ we shall experience what He experienced. We can't relate to someone and be compassionate about suffering or violence if we haven't experienced it ourselves. So I think the people who *have* experienced violence personally become much better people for that. They can empathize with the sufferers because they know what they have experienced.

'A couple of weeks ago in church there was a young girl who had gone through more than most people would ever expect to go through. Death would have been a great comfort to her, and yet, the moment she asked for death, Christ showed Himself to her on the Cross, and it was the visual contact she had with the crucified Christ that made her realize that her suffering was nothing compared with His. Now, although she is very profoundly handicapped, she is reaching out to others. Her sole attitude is to help other people, and she does it in such a fantastic way.

'I think what I'm trying to say, David, is that the

more we experience violence, the more we can become like Christ.'

'You mean something like Paul's reference to "the fellowship of Christ's sufferings"?'

'Exactly'

Janice
Speaking about the unspeakable

I asked my friend Janice to tell the story of a traumatic incident from her life. She is an interesting person in many respects, having been converted to Christianity from Judaism in her teens. The resulting estrangement from her family lasted many years. She went on to have a distinguished career as a missionary in India, but her life has been marked by a number of traumatic events and tragedies, of which the following account concerns only one. Janice tells her story in her own words, not only because she is a professional writer, but because the appalling nature of the event means that she alone can tell it.

I was lounging one day in front of the television, watching the regional news, when a brutal rape was reported. A photofit picture was shown on the screen of a man the local police wanted to interview in connection with the crime.

'I really don't understand it,' I said, shaking my head. 'It's outrageous what's going on nowadays.'

'What?' asked my husband, looking up from a car-maintenance manual. 'What don't you understand? What's dreadful?'

'It's dreadful that women can't go out alone at night. I remember coming in late one night from a prayer meeting and feeling quite anxious until I was actually indoors again. Mind you, if women hang around in pubs and clubs until closing time . . . well, they're asking for trouble, aren't they?'

He shrugged. 'Probably. I dunno. Oh, Janice, change the subject! Such things don't happen to the likes of us. By the way, what are we going to do about that old bed-settee?'

We had inherited the drab old thing from the previous owners of the house; obviously they hadn't wanted to take the horrible piece of furniture to their nice new home.

Next day, when my other half was at work, I telephoned the local newspaper and arranged for an advertisement to be placed in the Friday issue. It was to read as follows:

'Double bed-settee upholstered in sage-green dralon. No reasonable offer refused. Telephone . . .'

No one telephoned, either on the Friday or on the Saturday. We were out most of the Sunday, but then we would not have sold it on that day anyway.

'Well,' I shrugged, 'if no one buys that old settee by tomorrow, I'm going to phone the Council and ask them to take it away.' I did not care. I just wanted to get rid of the eyesore in our dining room.

Then, at eleven on Monday morning, the telephone rang. 'Hello,' came a man's well-spoken voice. 'Do you still have your bed-settee for sale? You do? Oh, that's great. May I come to see it? I'd be free during my lunch break. Will you be in?'

'Yes, yes. Please do come. About 12.30? Yes, sure, that'll be just fine,' I agreed, giving him detailed directions to our house.

A little before the agreed time, the doorbell chimed.

'Oh hello,' he said, offering his hand. 'I'm sorry if I'm a little early. I've come to see the bed-settee you have for sale.' Smartly-dressed, tall, well-built and handsome, he was probably only in his mid-to-late twenties. After shaking his hand, I ushered him through the hall into the dining room.

'What a most pleasant room,' he commented, walking to the French windows and looking out. 'You're obviously not overlooked by neighbours, are you?'

I shook my head. 'No, we're very secluded here. I'm quite pleased about that, because where we used to live . . . well . . . it was a little like being in a goldfish bowl.'

I directed his gaze away from the view of the garden back to the bed-settee.

'Ah yes, that's probably going to be ideal for what I need,' he replied, running his hand over the upholstery.

Suddenly, he jumped, asking about a banging noise which had occurred. I smiled, assuring him it was only air in the central heating pipes; a plumber was expected the next day to put it right. He sounded relieved, saying he'd thought there was someone else in the house. Slightly scared by his nervous reaction, I was beginning to wish there *was* someone else around.

'Well, are you interested in seeing the settee, Mr . . . er . . . Sorry, I didn't quite catch your name.'

He seemed absent-minded, volunteering nothing about himself, but asked if I would show him how the settee opened up into a double bed. Removing the two back cushions, I opened it out.

He looked delighted. 'Oh, that's just ideal for my purposes. May I sit on it?'

I nodded.

Then, quick as lightning, he roughly snatched at my right wrist and yanked me down onto him. Then he was on top of me. He was strong, much stronger than I could ever have imagined, leaving me with no hope of defending myself, preventing his violence or the rape which followed. I remember he kept yelling at me, shouting that I should not move or he would strangle me. I tried to kick, but he hit me harder, punching me, ripping at my clothing. I managed to claw his right cheek from his eye downwards. With his face over mine, he spat at me, then, having raped me, he pushed me aside and fled from the dining room, back into the hall, where he tidied his clothing. In no time, like a jack-rabbit, he was out of the front door.

Stunned, I fell from the bed-settee onto my hands and knees. My stomach gave a lurch and I felt violently sick. I felt dirty, and great racking sobs tore at my body. Somehow, I crawled upstairs to the bathroom. Tearing off my remaining clothes, I showered. Still feeling unclean, I stayed in the shower for at least an hour, maybe more. Drying myself, I put on my dressing-gown, bundled up my soiled, ripped clothes and took them out to the dustbin. Even handling the clothing made me feel dirty again; so I scrubbed my hands till they felt as sore as the rest of me.

'Oh, God, why, oh, why have You allowed this terrible thing to happen to me?' I yelled through my tears. 'What have I done to deserve this?'

Trying to harness my thoughts, I sat quietly for about ten minutes, mindlessly staring into space. Then it occurred to me – what if that man, that 'animal', as I named him, had passed on a sexually-transmitted disease? And then . . . what if I became pregnant? No! The full horror of what had happened, along with the possible consequences, was really hitting me hard. Maybe I needed a doctor. Yes, that's what I'd do. I'd phone our GP. William was a born-again Christian, and I thought he'd be kind and understanding. I telephoned his number, and he was with me within ten minutes.

The GP wanted to examine me, but I couldn't bear to be touched – not by him, not by a man . . . not by *any* man.

'Look, Janice, you really must go to the police about this matter. You cannot allow that man to get away with this . . . this terribly violent crime.'

I squinted at him through my bashed spectacles and shook my head. 'They'll think I'm thoroughly bad. They'll think I egged him on or something. After all, I did let him into the house. He came at my invitation.'

'Janice, oh, Janice, you must report it. Too many rapes go unreported and then these villains get away. Let me phone the police for you. You know I'll give you all the support I can.'

I thanked him. 'I know you will, William. You've always been so very kind . . . you, your family and most of the people at the church.'

He lowered his eyes, frowned and tightened his lips.

'What's wrong?' I asked.

'Nothing, Jan; well, not exactly. I just don't think it's wise to let any of the folk from the church know about what has happened. Some may not understand. Oh, and by the way, I certainly wish to keep this whole nasty matter away from my wife. I don't like her upset.'

'You don't like her upset? What about me? What do you think I'm like right now, or doesn't that matter?' I snapped.

His eyes bored into mine.

'Anyway, your wife is supposed to be my friend. And as for the Christians at the church . . . they've been like a family to me. I obviously wouldn't want to broadcast this attack to all and sundry, but if I don't have the support from God's family, then tell me, William, to whom *do* I turn?'

'You turn to God.'

'God and the police, eh?'

William was by then obviously getting very annoyed at my attitude. Leaving me, he went into the hall and telephoned the local constabulary.

About twenty minutes later a plain-clothed police officer, probably in his forties, arrived with a young woman police constable. They asked me, just briefly, what had happened. It was so desperately painful to describe.

'What have you done with your clothing?' asked the officer. I told him, and he walked out to the dustbin to collect it.

'No!' I screamed. 'I don't want the clothes to be brought back into the house. They're vile. They're . . .'

'I'm sorry, love, but forensic will need them. They'll also need to examine that bed-settee for . . . um . . . traces of him. By the way, you haven't showered or had a bath, have you?'

'Of course.'

The officer raised his eyes heavenwards, explaining that victims of rape should never shower. 'It doesn't help our case.'

Eventually, I accompanied them to the main police station in the town, where I made a statement. After having my fingerprints taken, I searched through pages and pages of mug-shots. Nothing. As they were attempting to make a photofit picture of what I thought the rapist looked like, my mind went blank. Did he have a long nose? Did he have blue, green or brown eyes? Sally, a young police officer, gave me a cup of tea.

'I'm sorry; this must be a terrible ordeal for you. I'm afraid it's going to be a long night. Soon I'll have to take you along to our photographer.'

'Why?'

'He'll have to photograph all your bruises and grazes.'

Feeling as thought I'd had enough, I looked at my watch. It was 2.35am and, bone-tired, all I wanted to do was to curl up in bed and just sleep and sleep.

Sally put her arm round me. 'Soon I'll have to accompany you to the doctor's room. The police surgeon is on his way. He'll need to give you a thorough examination, including an internal.'

I was adamant. No man – a stranger at that – was going to lay a finger on me. 'Please, Sally, take me home – now!'

'Hey, Janice, come on,' she said, putting her arm round me again.

'Get off! And don't 'Janice' me. I tell you I'm not going to be touched, and that's that. Don't you understand plain English? Now please take me home!'

Home again, I flopped into bed, but somehow sleep eluded me. I lay there in our prettily-decorated pink bedroom, staring at the ceiling, attempting to empty my brain of every troubling thought.

'Lord,' I prayed, 'give me the sleep I so need, please.'

I slept soundly for about eight-and-a-half hours until my husband woke me up. 'Sorry to disturb you, but the police think they have found your attacker. They need you to go back to the station to identify him. Sorry.'

I was just about to leave the house when the phone rang again. It was the duty sergeant; he informed me that the suspect in question had produced a watertight alibi. I had psyched myself up to face my attacker again, and all for nothing.

The following days – eventually weeks – were awful, bringing nothing but fear and anxiety, guilt and self-blame – if only I hadn't let a stranger into the house when I was all alone . . . Sleeplessness and flashbacks took over; the slightest little noise would startle me.

I couldn't attend the Sunday service, not did I attend the usual mid-week meeting. I didn't want to leave the house, face people and be sociable. Yet I hated staying in our home alone. William, the Christian doctor, visited me, and he felt I should go out and confront my fears head on. Despite all that, he still did not want either his own family or the family of God at the church to know about the rape.

'Why, William, are you so adamant regarding my keeping quiet? Surely, we are meant to bear one another's burdens, aren't we? And what if anyone comes here to the house, asking why I haven't been to the church? I'd have thought they're bound to miss me sooner or later. Anyway, it's not as though I've been immoral or anything. Honestly, you're treating me as if I were in some way responsible.'

William sighed, shaking his head. 'I think you've said enough, young lady!' he snapped.

Then I had to go to a special clinic at the General Hospital, which basically dealt with sexually-transmitted diseases. I felt ashamed and angry to be there, among prostitutes and those with HIV.

'We'll let you know the results of your tests in about a week,' reassured a nurse. 'I know it may seem an age away, but there we are. . . .'

I hoped upon hope my test results would be negative, and prayed fervently to God, pleading with Him not to allow me to be anything but healthy.

I was just leaving the hospital grounds when I saw Joanne, who regularly attended the same little church as I did. I tried to dart away, but it was too late; she had seen me.

'Hi, Jan, fancy seeing you here of all places. Oh dear, whatever have you been doing to yourself? You look as though you've been in the wars.'

I did not know what to say, for my face was still a bit of a mess. My eye was a real shiner. Joanne carried on, saying a lot of people at the church were wondering where I was. She told me I was conspicuous by my absence.

'Look, Joanne. I hope you won't be offended, but it has been suggested I keep quiet about what has been happening.'

Her eyes widened as she inspected my facial bruising. 'Don't tell me your husband did that!'

'No, of course not,' I replied, near to tears. 'As if he would! Oh, I wish I could talk to someone, but I can't.'

'Janice, we've been friends for quite a while now. I wouldn't want to intrude, but if you want a listening ear, then I'm available. Surely you can trust me. Anything you say I will keep in complete confidence.'

'Thanks, Joanne, but William doesn't want me to involve any of you.'

'Blow William,' she interrupted. 'You do what you want, OK? William doesn't own you. Would you like me to come home with you?'

I nodded.

Once home, I explained to her that I'd been unable to talk to anyone, except the police, about the rape. Even my husband and William didn't know all the gory details. When I tried to confide in Joanne, she asked me to stop, because it was all so horrible.

My attacker was eventually found by the CID. He

made the mistake of raping another woman in the neighbourhood soon after, and this led to his arrest.

For a number of years I was only too glad to let the whole thing sink into my subconscious mind. However, the mugging of Jane, a close personal friend, in a London street, made me realize that God's people are not immune from this kind of evil in a society where His laws are ignored. More recently, I have been able to think through my rape experience once again, and to wonder how many Christian women have suffered in silence, carrying a burden of guilt and shame, because there was no other believer able or willing to come alongside them and counsel them through it.

It is still a mystery to me that my doctor, now retired, imagined that his wife, and the little church to which I belonged, would be unable to come to terms with something like this. Was it their misunderstanding of Christian doctrine, or an unwillingness to believe that something so unsavoury could happen to someone in Christ? Why were they so helpless in the presence of happenings that were 'not nice'? Had they not read Paul's letter to the Galatians where he wrote, 'Carry each other's burdens, and in this way you will fulfil the law of Christ'? (Galatians 6:2). Perhaps, though, there were Christians among them who, had they known, *would* have come forward to help.

My husband and I, now living in Wales, are obviously no longer in membership at that Yorkshire church, and I feel the time has come to share with others my experience of something that, in the providence of God, ought not to happen, but does.

Joanne

His grace is sufficient

When I first met Joanne I saw a beautiful young woman, slim and fit looking, in her early thirties. She had two small children, twin girls, whom she and her husband had fostered as babies, and had very recently adopted. Beautiful she was, but there were shadows on her face, a weariness in her eyes, a sense of darkness about her. Describing how she felt at that time she says,

'There was a tremendous sense of relief. I was out of the fire, and so aware of how God was caring for me – for example, He had provided a house for us to live in. But I was in confusion, trying to decide the best way ahead, and I was dealing with all the emotions – swamped with the guilt – trying to cope with believing that marriage was so important.'

Joanne and Tom had met at a Bible College in Australia. Although they had come from different backgrounds, they felt suited as to their faith, and Tom especially asserted that God had led them together intending that they should marry.

'Tom was a very lovely person,' says Joanne, 'and we became good friends. We were teamed up to work together, and we got on. I hadn't felt romantic feelings, but he was someone I admired and respected. It was a very spiritual environment. Everything was spiritual-ized, and that can be confusing.'

'Looking back on it now, Joanne,' I asked, 'what were the first signs of Tom's odd behaviour?'

'The week before we got married I had the first inkling that there was some sort of irrational conduct, but when I discussed it with the minister it was all put down to pre-wedding nerves. I can't remember specifics, but Tom was fearful of something that was totally irrational. Then on our wedding day he was late – later than I was! And it was because he was paranoid about something on his suit and had to go back to the house and get it all wiped down.

'It was obvious even on the honeymoon, but I never thought seriously of mental health problems. And it wasn't every day, just once in a while. I had felt that this marriage was God's will and plan, so I tried to nor-malize things. The first bout of violence was a tremen-dous shock. It happened within the first three months. I could not believe what was happening. I remember such a sense of unreality, such a sense of shock. I locked myself in the bathroom, that first time, and hid behind the shower curtain, and sobbed, "God, what's going on here, what have I done, what have I said?"

'I felt that I had caused it, that I had said too much, obviously touched a nerve. I felt very responsible for it. Then, after a while, when I came out, he was very sorry and remorseful, and I really thought it wouldn't happen again.

'The second occasion when it happened, the threat-ening, the fists, the hitting, I became frightened and spoke to the minister about it. He was astounded and said he'd have a word with Tom, and that was it, nothing outside of that happened or was dealt with. I became very wary of how I spoke or what I did, because I felt guilty, responsible. Looking back I can see how he reinforced the idea that it was my fault by things that he said.

'Sometimes we could go for long spells without anything. And he could be so loving and appreciative of me; he'd swing from one extreme to the other. I had eight years of happy marriage really, given that we coped. I felt guilty, wary and nervous, but I never sat down and thought, 'Oh, I'm so unhappy!' We called it 'the hassle'. Tom said he was being hassled in his mind. We didn't talk about it much because it would aggravate it, but that was how it was referred to.'

After some years they settled in Scotland. Tom found work labouring on country estates. Joanne used her nurses' training in various convalescent homes, often driving long distances from their remote village.

Joanne can see, with the benefit of healing and hindsight, that Tom's behaviour was bizarre. But, at the time, she firmly believed herself to be somehow responsible. 'If only I could just do better,' she told herself, 'if I could get things right, he wouldn't be like this.'

'I hid the bruises. The first time I ever bought foundation, to try and cover it, I didn't think it worked very well. Usually he hit me where you couldn't see bruises, or he'd pin me against the wall by the neck. I was only bruised on my face a few times. I remember a couple of times going to work feeling ashamed, trying to wear my hair over my face. When people asked about the bruises I said, "Yea, that's Tom. He's my sparring partner, and he got a bit rough. It was in fun. We were mucking around." Friends became suspicious.'

During this time, Joanne and Tom fostered twin baby girls. Joanne believed that the children would help Tom to settle, to become more contented. And she found tremendous comfort in their love.

I asked Joanne to describe some of Tom's behaviour as his problems became more pronounced:

'He did abnormal things – cutting up his clothes because he had it in his head that there was something on them. One time we were in a boat on the river having a family picnic and he was wearing sunglasses. He got the idea that the sunglasses were soiled, so he just dropped them in the river. He was paranoid about chemicals being sprayed around us, about the ozone layer. I knew whenever there was a news item about Greenpeace activities, he would be worse for a while. But there were other things that set him off that I had no idea about, no warning at all.

'He wouldn't hug me or hold my hand in case I was contaminated, and he discouraged me from sitting beside him. Not in public, he knew how to behave in public. He would sit beside me in church and put his arm along my shoulders, but at home he'd say "Would you mind sitting over there." He wiped my arms and chest with a towel before hugging me. After a while I didn't look for hugs or to hold hands. He relied on verbal expressions of how he felt rather than expressing himself physically, but it became the norm. I accepted it and I loved him.'

Towards the end, though, Tom's abuse of Joanne was verbal. 'I was a b***** and a bitch. "You try that again and you'll get it twice as hard!" Little courtesies and things went right out the window. He was very demanding in terms of meals. I had to be at his beck and call, run his bath. He would say, "You know, I lay awake last night looking at you while you slept, and you are so ugly." He was ashamed of me. And my health was suffering, my appetite was gone, I didn't want to live. I used to get frightened when he came home, ready to defend myself and the children – not in the early days, but the last couple of years.'

I asked Joanne how her Christian faith supported her at that time.

'I think I really just kept believing that somewhere along the line it was going to resolve. There would be some kind of intervention, healing. It got complicated with the girls. I think I had a tremendous amount of guilt because the problem was evident when we got married and I was always trying to be better, and because we coped and we did have lots of happy times. I just believed in my heart that things were going to resolve. But six or eight months after the girls were placed with us, after we had bonded with them, I realized how inappropriate it was to have them in such a situation. I suppose I acted selfishly at the time because I wanted to hold on to them.

'At first I was happy because I didn't think anything unusual was happening. Then when I couldn't think that any more, I believed it would resolve. There was never a time when God wasn't there, part of my life. Eventually Tom lost his walk with God and tried to interrupt mine. I used to be haunted by the thought, "This is not what it's supposed to be about." As a Christian I really esteemed the marriage ideal. We'd been given these beautiful children – what was going on? Should I report this to the Social Services? And the Bible verse: "God requires a gentle, quiet spirit" – I used to hit myself over the head with that all the time when I felt that I'd aggravated the situation.'

'So, Joanne, you felt that you had two people upset with you instead of just one: God *and* your husband?'

'Oh, yes.'

So despite her faith, Joanne was confused into believing that *she* was at fault, that she should keep trying harder to please her husband, that he was justified in his treatment of her. This is a not uncommon response in the thinking of the abuse victim; we should be perfect, and if we are not, we deserve what happens to us. It is as if we are in opposition to the Bible message of God's unconditional love: we believe all love to be conditional, and somehow we must meet every condition.

There were people who could see what was happening to Joanne, who cared about her and wondered how they could help. Her mother, living a long distance away and only visiting rarely, left after one visit feeling deeply concerned at her son-in-law's treatment of her daughter. In the early days he had kept his behaviour towards her well hidden from others, but gradually it became more and more normal in his mind, and he no longer felt a need to disguise it. Joanne's mother realized that things were far from good, and her prayers for her daughter became more fervent.

As Joanne describes those years, she is anxious to reiterate the fact that, for the first eight years, she would not describe her marriage as unhappy.

'The first eight years, there were traumas, shocks, confusion. Yes, there was this sort of niggling thing, undercurrent of unrest, but nothing that made me feel miserable or that Tom and I wouldn't be together forever. I was happy, even though the physical abuse started three months into the marriage. But worse than the physical were the bizarre behaviours such as, after I had done all the ironing, I had to rewash everything because he felt it was dirty. He constantly washed his hands and wouldn't use a towel twice, so he went through every flannel, towel, even ironed clothing. He made a tremendous amount of work for me. And then there were the irresponsible things he did. He began to disregard other people's property. He would not turn up at work. He lost his reputation for being a good, reliable worker. He mismanaged money; borrowed things and didn't look after them; then I'd have to find them and return them. It was very difficult, and there was always the threat of strange things I might not be able to deal with.'

'Mummy, Mummy, we will protect you from Daddy,' cried the twins one day, when they saw Tom coming downstairs towards Joanne in anger. By then they were three years old. Their words served to awaken Joanne from the stupor into which the abuse had pushed her. Maternal feelings for the protection of her girls stepped in where self-preservation had failed, awakening her to the dangers of their situation.

'After all,' she realized, 'he may not hurt them physically now, but the day will come when he sees them as young women, and then perhaps he will feel about them as he does me. Also, it is terrible that they are living in fear of what he might do to me, their mother. They should not have to live in fear for me, and be thinking of ways to protect me. They should not have to see these things.' One time when Tom had struck her so hard that she had slammed up against a wall, she had looked up to see the terrified faces of her little ones, and her heart had contracted for them. Any hurt or damage to her was damaging them, too.

Joanne tells of one significant time when she really thought she was not going to survive. Afterwards she was alone in her room, and although she had prayed endlessly about it all before, this time, as she gave up the whole situation to God, she felt it was different. Out of an awareness of the absolute hopelessness of her problem, she unloaded it all unreservedly, completely, onto her heavenly Father.

'To me, it was an absolute point of the situation changing when I sat on the bed and dumped it all in God's lap. "There's nothing else I can do, if You don't do anything, this is it."

'That was just a couple of weeks before a visit from my mother. I remember it was September, and Mum asked me straight out what was happening, and it was the first time I had ever told anyone, and it was such a relief. Then I talked to a Christian friend who lived nearby, and who had seen it all along and been praying for me. Suddenly there was prayer support from other places.'

For Joanne, it all moved quite quickly after that. In the January a friend from their Christian fellowship in Australia came to stay for two weeks. She grasped the situation immediately. She felt impressed to offer Tom a return air ticket to Australia, and she contacted a pastor in Australia to explain to him the care Tom needed. This account does not allow room for all the details of his departure: how often he changed his mind; how he nearly missed his flight; how God's intervention became obvious to Joanne and those looking on. In the March Tom left for Australia, and Joanne took the girls to visit her mother for a while. She applied for housing near her mother, and was told that it would be years before any would be available. But within two weeks, back in Scotland, she and her friend were on their knees praying for the housing situation when the call came through to say that a house was ready for her.

And suddenly she was living in a lovely house, near her mother, with family and church prayer support.

As she talked with Christian friends, the dark cloud

in which she seemed to live assumed an identity: guilt. Guilt possessed her from every angle. She felt she had failed as a wife to please her husband and keep him happy with her. All the reasons she has already described for feeling guilty came to the surface.

Joanne now takes up the story of how she came out of that time of darkness:

'I think, for me, it was just a tremendous sense that God still loved me despite the fact that I was letting my marriage go. He just put into my heart, "My grace is sufficient for you." It was so real. I had had a sense of guilt that I had no other choice but to go back to the situation in order to please God. Then there was the sense of release to know that God loved me no matter what I did. I had never thought of divorce as an option ever. The marriage ideal was in stone. But I had come to the point where I would have preferred Jesus to have taken me than to have gone back into that situation. Death was the only way to get out of it without guilt. I was not suicidal; but a car accident or whatever. It had appeared the only way to escape, to take the responsibility off me. So it was like this huge light switching on inside. God saying, "My love doesn't change. I am not going to turn my back on you."

'The people at the church I began attending were so kind and supportive. Nobody said, "You should go back; that's what is required of you." Nobody said anything like that. It was a tremendous help.'

Joanne did still experience pressure to continue in the marriage. The friends in Australia tried to persuade her to go over there. Tom was convincing them that there was nothing wrong. She had been honest with him, and given him her address, because she felt that was right, and he had a return ticket for a year. It was frightening to think what might happen if he had come back.

'Certainly for a good year or so after he was there he reinforced the idea that I was the one who had a problem. I needed to get my act together, and he was very spiritual and there was lots of preaching; the same things I had used to preach to myself; the things I believed in about marriage and the family, etc.'

Joanne finishes the story herself:

'God has shown me that He loves me and that I don't have to return to that situation. It became clear to me how God had led; taken Tom right away from us to the other side of the world. He found the house for us, and that reinforced what I was experiencing in my heart, in my spirit, that God does love me; that I wasn't required to go back into that situation in order to please Him.'

'*Joanne, My grace is sufficient for thee. . . .*'

Ken
Grace and forgiveness

*'He hung on that cross for the sins of mankind
He had no one to turn to, He just hung there and died
I thank you, Lord Jesus, for what you have done
For through your resurrection I'm one of God's sons.'*
From *Atonement* by Alan Fraser

Sunday 10 December 1978. We all have dates imprinted on our minds and easily recalled. This date is memorable for me, because on the evening of that day I was stabbed by a mugger on my way home from a church service. In the morning, before leaving for church, I had completed reading R. T. France's book, *The Living God*, in which I had read these words: *'But God too has entered into a commitment that He will be their God, that He will stand by them, dwell among them, lead them and watch over them with His special favour.'* Late that night I was barely alive in a hospital emergency room, having been stabbed several times in an apparently random, financially-motivated mugging.

Much has been written about the relationship between suffering and a God of love. It is not my intention to offer anything new on the subject, simply to describe my own experience of suffering (as a reasonably innocent person), and to describe some of my own responses to it.

In December 1978 I was midway through a teacher-training course at Aberdeen College of Further Education (now Northern College). My subject was Religious Education. After completing an Honours degree in Religious Studies at Aberdeen University, I had drifted somewhat into the college course, as I really had no idea what I wanted to do career-wise. My somewhat less than spiritual plan was to take what would amount to little more than a year out (the grants were more generous in those days and I was on a full one!). I would then perhaps develop a clearer picture of what I wanted to do with my life.

I had been attending Gilcomston South Church of Scotland for several years. In December 1978 William Still was only thirty-three years into his marathon ministry. I was one of the large number of students who faithfully attended the morning and evening services, both of legendary duration.

On the date in question, the service began at 7pm and, as usual, finished about 9pm. Thereafter, as was customary, tea and coffee were served within the church building and most folk remained to talk with one another or speak to Mr Still. I was often one of the last people to leave the building, being of a fairly talkative nature! That evening I left Gilcomston at around 10.25pm to walk back to my flat alone. For several months I had shared a flat with Harry Smart, who at the time was a youth missioner in the Bon Accord Free Church on Rosemount. The flat was at the rear of the church, and the shortest route to the door from Gilcomston involved, in the latter stages, walking down some steps into a dark grassy area bordered by a primary school, the back of some tenements and some distant flats. Street lighting existed but was rather faint. It was my usual route home, but I had always approached it with a degree of trepidation. Coming from the Isle of Rhum – population twenty-five – I had what I always reckoned to be a realistic view of the dangers of city life. However, I always felt it would be unacceptably cowardly of me to take the longer way round by a busier street to reach the flat.

That Sunday evening was no different. I reached the foot of the fifty or so steps and began walking along the pavement towards the rear of the church where the flat was situated. On my left was the road, the other side of which was the open grassy area. To my right was the high wall which ran along the back gardens of the tenements. I had walked about ten yards when I saw a man come round the corner of the church about thirty yards ahead, to the right. He began to walk down the middle of the road towards me, staggering slightly. Of course, I became slightly more apprehensive but, as always, I dismissed my fears with the argument that I had met many people in such situations before, with nothing untoward resulting!

The following point I did not mention in the subsequent trial, as it perhaps may have appeared too far-fetched, but as the chap approached, my head was actually turned to the right. I was trying to make out if there was any chink of light to be seen behind the curtains of my flat. This would tell me if my flatmate was at home. Turning my head, however, was actually also a conscious decision on my part, the purpose being to show the man on the street how relaxed I was about his presence and to force myself to adopt an air of casualness.

Then, very quickly, I was aware of two things. The man who had been on the road a second before was now towering in front of me. Secondly, I was experiencing a strange, unfamiliar sensation of weakness and a draining of energy. I looked down, and in the weak light of the street lamps I saw with horror a knife with an enormous blade being gripped firmly in the left hand of the stranger who had now become my assailant. I experienced a surge of sheer panic, but it passed in a flash. My mind then remained very clear throughout the incident. I firmly believe that this self-control in the dire circumstances in which I stood, was a gift of God. Of that I am convinced. I am by nature a pure coward, unblemished by any hint of courage! That I was able to remain alert and to form plans was nothing short of miraculous. I know that others, both Christian and non-Christian, have had the same experience, and I believe it is probably a gift which God has written into the natural order. Another aspect of the event was that for about 15 to 20 minutes I felt no pain – none at all. This helped my brain to concentrate on working on a plan to escape from the situation.

Almost immediately, my assailant said, 'Money'. I had none but, hoping he might think it to be a nice fat wallet, I offered him the little pocket Bible I had taken to church. He took it from me, muttered 'Bible', and threw it aside. I then said, 'My flat is just there. Let me go in and I'll get you some money.' Clutching at straws, I know, but I had the intention, of course, of trying to close the door behind me.

'Na, na, na,' was the response.

I then pushed my attacker and tried to run. I fell immediately onto the road. As I learned later, some muscles affecting the working of my left leg had been cut through. My assailant then cut me on the neck with the knife. I stood up, grappling with him, holding onto the wrist which held the knife and shouting for help. My attacker stopped hitting me and grabbed my throat.

Again I pushed my assailant and tried to run. This time I did not fall. I ran across the grassy area, and at its far end I turned to see what the chap was up to. He was simply standing where I had left him. It was only later that I learned that he had been cut quite badly with his own knife during our struggle.

I ran – staggered rather – up a short hill called Jack's Brae into Northfield Place. I stood in the middle of the road there and shouted a number of times: 'Help! I've been stabbed. Somebody please fetch an ambulance.' No one came out to me, though I saw a few twitching curtains and no doubt some phone calls were made.

A middle-aged man putting out rubbish bags about fifteen yards away looked at me and went inside his tenement block. I knew I had to get help fast as I was losing a lot of blood; so I set off along the pavement on the right-hand side of the street, bent double, clutching my midriff. A young couple met me on the pavement but stepped onto the road to let me pass. They really could not have failed to notice the trail of blood I was leaving. At the end of the street I was close to total collapse. I was very faint and it was becoming difficult for me to remain on my feet. I remember very clearly leaning over the bonnet of a white car and leaving a mess of blood on it. I have no idea what would have gone through the mind of the owner in the morning!

While I was leaning on the car, an elderly couple crossed the street towards me. They were on their way home from a social evening. They did not hesitate. They took my arms and led me to some steps where I sat and was held by a man who had come out of a flat. While I was sitting there, literally watching my blood draining out of me, from one step onto another, running onto the pavement, I thought I was going to die. I said to the chap holding me up, 'I think I'm going.' What I found most interesting and intriguing for myself was that I felt no fear at all, and I was only just beginning to feel some pain. I heard someone say, 'His throat's cut as well!' I had a small cut on my neck which required a few stitches, but with all the blood it no doubt looked worse at that time.

Police and ambulance duly arrived, and I was taken to Accident and Emergency, where I was operated on during the night. I recall the anaesthetist saying to me, as I was about to have a needle stuck into my arm, 'This may hurt a bit.' I remember saying to him, 'You must be joking!'

I awoke the next day with a large number of tubes attached to me, but otherwise I really felt fine. My parents were there, and other friends came by during the day, though they were not able to speak to me. I spent much of the day asleep, though I was interviewed by the police, who told me that my assailant had been picked up soon after the attack and that he was known to them as a local hard man, who was trying to build a reputation in the area. Also that he was not long out of prison.

The trial of my attacker, Alan Fraser, took place over two days in May 1979. Fraser was defended by Donald Findlay QC. The trial was an interesting experience throughout, and it was rather intriguing to be described as a 'liar' and a 'Jekyll and Hyde character' by Mr Findlay! The defence case was that I had attacked Fraser with a group of friends in revenge for a fight I had lost in an Aberdeen pub (which I'd never heard of) several weeks previously. Fraser had picked up the knife in order to throw it away and I had run on to it. A number of my friends were put on the witness stand to testify to my sound character. Fortunately I managed to slip through that test! My flatmate, Harry, was asked about my interests. In his reply he said, 'Well, he is a Christian, though I wouldn't really describe it as an interest!'

At the conclusion of the trial, my attacker was found guilty and sentenced to eight years for attempted murder. Lord Cowie, the presiding judge, said in his summing up: 'No words of mine can describe the revulsion I feel for your behaviour. It is incredible that normal, law-abiding citizens of Aberdeen cannot go about their business without being subjected to an attack of this sort.'

While Fraser was being led away, I overheard (I was probably meant to hear) one of his friends saying to another, 'God help that bloke when Alan gets out!'

As I was leaving the court with my friends, I saw the press waiting at the entrance. During the trial such headlines as 'Bible Youth Tells of Stab Ordeal' had already appeared, and the press wanted to know my reaction to the verdict and sentence. 'What are your views on human nature now?' asked one reporter. I replied something to the effect that what had happened to me had served to confirm my views on human nature. I was asked how I felt towards my attacker. I replied that I felt no animosity towards him; that I felt sorry for him in that he was of a mind to commit such an act, and that I was sorry that he did not realize there was a better sort of life than he was living.

I had been aware that I would be interviewed by the press and I really wanted to be careful in what I said. I had no desire to use the occasion for simplistic or tub-thumping evangelism. At the same time I *did* want to communicate the fact that as a Christian I forgave my attacker and that the better way of living to which I referred would clearly mean the Christian way.

The whole business of forgiveness is complex. On one level, the teaching of Jesus is very clear, 'Forgive your enemies – seventy times seven.' On the other hand, I wondered then, as I still do, about the correlation between forgiveness and repentance. To become a Christian one must repent of one's sins and acknowledge one's need for the atoning sacrifice of Christ.

Repentance is a prerequisite of forgiveness, but I still found it easy to forgive my assailant. Why? Firstly, because at the simple level the Bible obliges us to. Forgiving those who have wronged us is not optional but mandatory. Frequently, we see in our papers the effects of grudge-bearing and revenge-seeking. A corrosive, self-destroying bitterness may develop, and that does no one any good, with ourselves, our families and friends perhaps all being hurt by our thirst for revenge. And if some kind of retaliation is achieved, what then? Further retaliation from the other party, no doubt with the stakes being raised each time. So forgiveness becomes not only an appropriate response to the biblical injunction, but the most mature and sensible method of dealing with hurt at the practical level.

Secondly, I found it easy to exercise forgiveness in my situation because of the amount of good which arose out of the experience! It is generally accepted that good may arise from evil events. Personal experience of bereavement may help one to sympathize more meaningfully with another who is undergoing the same experience and so on.

So what 'good' did my stabbing lead to?

● In December 1978 I was in a state of personal turmoil. As I said at the beginning, part of this turmoil was due to the fact that I had drifted into the College of Further Education with little thought being given to the future. I really had no idea what I wanted to do with my life. I was drifting through the college course, making little effort and utterly *under*whelmed at the idea of being a teacher. The stabbing stopped me dead (almost!) in my tracks, and gave me the impulse and time to take stock and reassess the direction in which my life was going. This resulted in my becoming much more focused regarding my future plans.

• I found myself *over*whelmed by the support and love I was shown by family and friends! I would sometimes have two dozen friends queuing to see me at visiting time in hospital and I received innumerable cards and letters from more distant friends. At a time when I really needed it most, I was presented with a fantastic demonstration of love and affection. I am sure that all those people cannot know the extent to which their visits were a huge boost to my physical and spiritual healing.

• I was visited on a number of occasions by a certain young – exceptionally pretty – female student by the name of Donna from the College of Education. Sometimes she came with a group, sometimes on her own. I knew Donna slightly from attending the college Christian Union and from church; and even before the stabbing it was becoming increasingly a pleasure to be in her company, as she had personality and wit to match her looks! In brief, not long after I left hospital we began a relationship which resulted in marriage in 1983. (Twenty years after we began going together, she would not forgive me if I did not affirm that she still retains her personality, wit and good looks!) Had Donna not visited me in hospital and left me a card which indicated her affection for me, our relationship may not have resulted.

● The entire experience of being mugged, stabbed and being so close to death is an utterly fascinating experience to have had. I value tremendously the lessons I have learned from it. I always liked to regard myself as an adventurous kind of person, and even during the experience, as I was running away from the scene, I recall clearly thinking, 'This is exciting!' I found it intriguing that, as others have found in similar situations, I had no fear of dying and indeed felt no pain at all for quite some time after being stabbed. I do not wish this to sound clichéd, but I really found it to be the case that God's grace was sufficient to deal with the situation.

● Finally, and perhaps most significantly of all, Fraser's arrest and conviction were the beginning of a chain of events which led to his becoming a Christian several years later while still in prison. I am sure that the prayers of myself, my church and others played their part in this. Fraser has told his story elsewhere in the book, *And You Visited Me*. It relates the work of the Scottish Prison Christian Fellowship and the testimonies of former prisoners who have become Christians. Without question, Fraser's story is an amazing demonstration of the power of God to change lives, perhaps especially those who seem beyond the reach of human agencies. As Fraser once said to me, 'I was visited by social workers, psychologists and the rest but they did me no good. What changed me was hearing the Christian Gospel.' The lines at the start of this essay are from a poem, *Atonement*, which was written by Fraser while still in prison.

In August 1984, several years after the trial and Fraser's imprisonment, Donna and I were preparing tea

in our flat when the doorbell rang. We went to the door
and, according to Donna, I went white. She did not
immediately know why. On the doorstep stood Alan
Fraser who, as far as I knew, was still in prison. He
shifted nervously on his feet and, looking just above my
head, began a speech he'd obviously carefully prepared.
In it he said he had come to apologize for stabbing me
and to ask for my forgiveness. He explained that he had
become a Christian two years earlier in prison and that
his life was completely changed. I had composed myself
while Fraser was speaking, and when he finished I
immediately held out my hand which he shook firmly.
He told me later he had been very nervous about how I
would respond to his turning up on my doorstep! I
invited him in and we sat and talked for some time.

As Fraser was actually still serving his sentence, he
had to return to prison at a certain time. He was out
during the day on a 'Training for Freedom' scheme. As
he left, we arranged for him to come round again the
following evening. I have to admit to a certain apprehensiveness when he was standing making his speech
on the doorstep. Donna and I had heard that he had
become a Christian (through a friend who was in the
Prison Christian Fellowship), but having the chap who
had stabbed and almost killed me standing in front of
me did make the heart beat a little faster! However, I
have to say, both on that first occasion, and when he
returned the next evening, dressed in a suit and bear-
ing a gift, I was overwhelmed by the change I saw in
him. I had only ever seen him on three previous occasions: when he attacked me, at an identity parade, and
in court. There he had been aloof, callous, uncaring and
cruel. Now here was a man out of whose eyes shone a
profound love for God and people. What a complete
transformation! Alan Fraser was bursting with enthusi-

asm for his new-found faith, and possessed a desire both to grow in it and to share it with others.

Fraser told me about the nightmares he had endured for years in prison on account of his attack on me. He had been in prison on a number of occasions, but that was the first time he had attacked someone with a knife. He had spent years blaming others for his plight – his parents, the police and even me for coming along the road at that particular time! He had been advised by people inside that it would look good on his record if he started attending Christian meetings in the prison, so he did. At first he made fun of the Christians who took the meetings, but he began to be very impressed with the folk from the Prison Christian Fellowship. Then he began to realize that he couldn't keep on blaming everyone else for his guilt. He confessed his sins to God and asked Christ into his life. After that he told me it was as if he were on cloud nine for a fortnight! He felt like a new person.

Some years later, Alan invited me to Craiginches Prison in Aberdeen as he was then a member of the Prison Christian Fellowship. He was to lead a service of worship. Sitting in a semicircle with the prisoners, he invited me to relate what had happened to me as a victim of crime and how I believed God had helped me. He then told the story of the mugger who had attacked me and what had subsequently become of him. He then said, 'And in case you're wondering how come I know so much about this chap – it's me!'

The faces of the prisoners were indeed a picture! There was a brief moment of silence, followed by several of them asking incredulously how we could now be sitting side by side in a church service. It was a tremendous opportunity to speak about forgiveness and the life-changing impact of the Christian message.

Alan and I see each other on an irregular basis. We have spoken at each other's churches about our shared experience, and our families get together for meals. Donna and I were surprise guests at Alan's 40th birthday party and Alan and his wife came to mine.

In another twist to our story, the police forensic scientist whose evidence was the clinching factor in Alan's being found guilty is a Christian friend. During my 40th birthday party I saw Alan's wife, Grace, looking at the three of us chatting in the middle of the hall. She remarked on how unusual the situation was!

Two of our daughters are soon to go for a sleep-over with Alan's daughters. Alan has offered to help me complete the laying of slabs for a path I'm struggling with in our back garden – an offer I fully intend to accept!

My experiences of being a victim of a mugging and Alan's subsequent conversion have convinced me that – without question – forgiveness is an infinitely preferable option to bitterness or a desire for revenge. In summary, these events have shown me • the reality of the power of God in extreme circumstances and • the reality of the transforming power of the Christian Gospel.

Mollie

In the right place
at the right time

My search for understanding and insights took me to the town of Stirling, in Scotland.

Stirling is a place I like, and have done since I first went there many years ago as a 9-year-old tourist. I like the way it is stiff with history. Bannockburn is not far away, and there is a huge monument on a hill across the River Forth to the Scottish patriot William Wallace. I love its setting, too, the town lapping the base of the Castle Rock, which towers over the flat valley of the Forth with a vast procession of mountains beyond. You can look up from the pavement almost anywhere in the town and see green hills or dark mountains. 'I will lift up mine eyes unto the hills,' said the Psalmist. You can do that in Stirling.

Yet there are, of course, tough deprived estates in Stirling as there are in most large towns; and on one of these estates lived an embittered loner called Thomas Hamilton. One March morning in 1996, Hamilton took some guns (which he held legally), slung them into the back of a grubby van and drove to the picturesque little town of Dunblane, just a few miles to the north. There he walked into a primary school and gunned down most of a class of infants, together with their teacher. Most of the children were killed outright, and the few survivors were seriously injured. Hamilton then killed himself. The event shocked the world and impinged upon the lives of thousands of people living in the area, not least the life of a woman called Mollie, the then co-ordinator of Victim Support Stirling, whom I had come to interview.

Mollie welcomed me to her council house in a village in the hills above Stirling. I knew little about her, beyond knowing that she had a story to tell. She turned out to be a smallish, grandmotherly figure in, I suppose, her sixties. Her house is comfortably furnished, and neater and tidier than the homes of those who are deeply involved in voluntary work often are. She is gently spoken and you can imagine people pouring out their hearts to her. You can also sense that she is a person who won't stand any nonsense.

She is deeply involved in church life, so it comes as a surprise to discover that it is only recently that she became a committed Christian. She went to church as a child and attended Sunday School, but then, when she was eighteen, she drifted away from the church, as people do, and stayed away till she was fifty. About that time there were a couple of tragedies in the family, and these prompted not Mollie, but her husband Sam, to return to church. His family had had lifelong connections with the Methodist Church in Stirling and so it was to that church that he returned. Somehow, the minister's preaching spoke to him in a very helpful way, and he suggested to Mollie that she should come as well, which she did. She found it difficult going back to church after more than thirty years. Church had changed in that time, become unfamiliar, but Mollie coped by being quiet, and listening and observing.

She went to church like this for about eight years. 'During that eight-year period,' she said, 'I believed that the Lord had never let me go. Although I'd moved away from church, the Lord had never let go of me, and I can see that very clearly now, because I've had 'lamp-post' experiences all the way through my life.' She had, however, begun to realize that there was something missing, something that she hadn't done. She had Christian friends who had something that she wanted and did not have.

At about that time, the Reverend Rob Frost arrived in Stirling with a mission team, to conduct an evangelistic campaign based on the Methodist Church. Rob is a man small of stature but of great evangelistic zeal, gifts and energy. He is the founder of a big Christian jamboree called Easter People, author of many books and initiator of many mission projects. Mollie just knew him as 'wee Robbie'. The little church hummed with activity and, among other things, members were asked to go knocking on doors. Mollie volunteered, but as she sat there in the training session, she thought, 'I've no right to go out knocking on anyone's door because I'm not a committed Christian.'

Mollie went away, sought out some Christian friends, and explained the situation to them. They lovingly supported her over the next few days, and she accepted Jesus at that time.

'That's approximately six years ago,' she said, 'and I regret very much the time that I spent away, but the amazing thing is that the Lord has been able to teach me as much as He has in that short period of time. The more I learn, the more I realize how much there is to learn!'

It was not long before God found this very forthright, active person something to do, because only a few weeks later, a plea for help went out from Central Scotland Police, who were asking for volunteers to help support victims of crime. Sam and Mollie had been prison visitors for a number of years, which had given Mollie some knowledge of offenders and victims, and now that Sam was having to withdraw from that work through ill-health, it seemed the right time to move on. Mollie offered her services, passed their selection procedures, and embarked upon a three-month training course to be a worker with Victim Support. It proved rather an unhappy experience at first.

'We had absolutely excellent trainers,' she recalls, 'and the difficulty wasn't with them; it was with me. I felt at times that I was being stretched almost beyond my limits, and I would come home on a Monday evening and say to Sam, "You know, I don't think this is for me. I maybe don't want to go back next week." '

There is a saying that behind every good man there is a good woman. It often operates the other way round too: behind many good woman there is a good man. In Mollie's case, it is her husband who is a great encourager, and on that occasion he replied, 'Well, I think you should finish the training and then you'll know if you're able to do it or not.' So Mollie carried on, and was stupefied when, at the end of the course, they came to her and asked if she would like to become the first Co-ordinator of Victim Support Stirling!

'I could not believe it,' says Mollie. 'I spent that entire day – how can I describe it? – wrapped in cotton wool, because I felt that this was God's work that I was embarking upon, and that He was going to use me in that work. While I was sitting in the Sheriff Court café that afternoon, I remember hearing a voice say clearly,

"This is what all the experiences of your life have been about." It was almost as if all the difficult experiences of my life (some of them crimes themselves) had been brought together into this one situation. I think even at that early stage I recognized just how important it was, not only to start as the Co-ordinator, but to establish a very firm base. I knew instinctively this was not something that could be done in a way that you sometimes find in the voluntary sector, where you don't have to commit yourself totally. This was about working every hour that God sends. I worked for three years as Co-ordinator, and it took every minute of that time to get it established.' In the light of subsequent events, it became clear how vital it was that Mollie had that core group established, and a very firm base from which to operate.

The organization with which Mollie had become involved, called 'Victim Support', was started by two women in the city of Bristol in the early 1970s. They had both been victims of crimes which were reported in the local press, and one of the women realized that the other would be feeling just as bad about it as she was herself. So she went to see the other woman.

'I was the other person mentioned in the same article,' she said, 'and I thought I'd just come down and see how you are.' Victim Support grew out of this simple contact, and spread steadily in England and Wales. Then, in 1984, it gained a foothold in Scotland. Some pensioners living in the tough industrial town of Coatbridge had been victims of violent crime in their area. Recognizing how badly upset they all were, and having read about the Bristol Victim Support Group, they invited Victim Support to come to Coatbridge – and thus was established the first such group in Scotland.

The stage has now been reached when virtually every

town in that country is covered. It is simply a voluntary organization supporting victims of crime. Virtually all of its workers, apart from some paid staff at national level, are volunteers. To Mollie, this is very important: 'We aren't paid personnel going out from some official organization,' she says. 'We are just representatives of our community, if you like, who are saying to the victims, "We've come to see how you are." '

'What sort of people come seeking help?' I asked. 'Obviously they'll have come from all walks of life, but what sorts of crimes have they experienced?'

'Right from the first years, Victim Support in Stirling was given every category of crime,' she replied, 'and that included everything from vandalism to murder. As you say, the victims come from all walks of life, but the referrals are made by the police. That is, provided the police at the scene of the crime have decided that someone from Victim Support should call. If the 'victim' at that stage opts out and says he or she doesn't want anyone to call, the police will tell us that, though we might at that stage still send a letter. If the victim does not opt out, then we automatically contact him or her. It could be by telephone at the initial stage to arrange a meeting if such is necessary. But sometimes, with the more serious crimes, we don't make a phone call; we go straight to the victim's home and make contact that way.'

At this point in our conversation I began to experience something like pangs of conscience. I had turned down an offer of help from Victim Support shortly after my own mugging, and I was now beginning to realize that this may have slowed down my recovery. I had already written my own experience for the first story of this book, but, as a result of my conversation with Mollie, I decided to rewrite it; to be a little less 'triumphalistic' and rather more honest. I wondered if a lot of people (like me) said, 'No thanks'.

'Yes,' said Mollie. 'It's quite interesting, though. The experience of most of the visitors is that when they get to the door, the "victim" (for want of a better word) will say, "Oh, I'm fine, thank you very much. I don't need any help. Mind you, I'm very angry." And before long he's said, "You'd better just come in, and I'll tell you how angry I am." An hour and a half later, you're still there. And you listen. What we do find is that the crime committed is usually the straw that breaks the camel's back. Very often it unlocks the rest of the things that are going on in the person's life; and so you can become a real listening ear for hurts or family difficulties or whatever, and he'll use that time with you to talk through whatever problems he has.'

If non-intrusiveness is an important principle, so is confidentiality. Although Mollie can talk interestingly for hours about her work, personal anecdotes and case histories are rather sparse. This is because volunteers are carefully trained not to break confidences, not even to the co-ordinator, without permission from the victim. There are, however, cases where this rule must be broken. Sometimes victims themselves 'breathe out threatenings and slaughter' against their assailants. Most often the visitor knows that this is just words, a reflection of how the victim feels; but there is the odd occasion when the victim means it. Mollie herself can recall a case where the victim said he had a knife: 'I had to report that one,' she says. The same applies when child sex abuse is involved; but the reporting never happens without the victim's being told.

The victim is also told in any case where there is a need for referral to another organization. Mollie makes it clear that they are very much a referral organization.

'We are normally with the victim within forty hours after the crime has been committed, and then we stay with the victim until he or she is able to move on. However, if there are some lingering problems or re-surfacing hurts from long ago, it would be our job to refer victims on to the correct organizations, always with their knowledge and permission. The victims themselves dictate how we help, if in fact we do.'

Referral may often be necessary to help the victim not to 'cling' to the visitor. Some victims are lonely peo-ple, who inevitably want to adopt their friendly, caring, Victim Support worker as their best friend, becoming perhaps quite demanding in their need, and being most reluctant to let their new-found friend go. (Ministers also know this problem well!) In such cases it has to be firmly, but gently, explained to the person that the vis-itor has many other people who need his or her help, and the visits cannot go on for ever. One elderly lady, Mollie recalls, had been a victim of burglary, and really was not wanting the visitor to move out of her life, because she was intensely lonely. Victim Support managed to encourage her to go to a meeting held in a local hall. Because she was too timid to go down by herself, a worker took her to the meeting, introduced her and sat with her for a while. Next time, she was able to go by herself.

The way victims react to violence varies enormously in terms of the severity of the symptoms they display, the length of time the symptoms persist, the time when the symptoms first surface, and the stages the victims pass through.

The nature of the symptoms themselves also varies. Some victims blot out the event, like a family whose shop was raided by an armed man, and who afterwards tried to carry on as if it had not happened. For others, there may be forgetfulness, sickness, headaches, night-mares, or the vivid 'relivings' of the traumatic event which are termed 'flashbacks'. Mollie has also discovered that there is not always a close correspondence between the severity of the crime and the severity of the symptoms experienced. She gave an example of an elderly man whose car had been vandalized. For most people this would have been little more than a nuisance, but he seemed devastated by it; so the police in attendance called in Victim Support. The visitor discovered that the gentleman had lost his wife only six weeks earlier. During that period, he had been staying with his daughter, but had moved back into his house only the night before the car was vandalized. The visitor offered him a listening ear, and he was able to speak about his wife, and of how happy they had been in their married life. Photographs were brought out and the visitor went through them with him, helping thereby to ease some of the pain.

The severity of the symptoms and the quickness of recovery seem to depend, in part, on the victim's life, and whether or not he is happy, secure and fulfilled. For someone whose circumstances are not happy, where there have been other experiences of violence, or there is loneliness or bereavement, even a small trauma can be the last straw.

The time when their case comes to court can be a difficult and traumatic time for victims. 'Some people,' said Mollie, 'who have been very severely hurt, are accompanied to court, which is also part of our work, and have come out of court thinking, "Well, that's not going to interfere with the rest of my life," and in fact they've moved on very quickly into their life again and picked up the threads. But for others it's devastating.'

The only time Mollie displayed any anger in the

course of a long interview, was when she spoke of the effects on some victims of inappropriate, over-lenient sentences, or of assailants being discharged to go back and live near the victims they so terrified. This is surely an issue that society must address.

All things considered, Mollie believes that the hardest thing 'is the acceptance that your life can never be exactly the same as it was five minutes before the crime occurred. In particular, I'm thinking about murder victims and their families. Obviously, what people most want to happen is that they will be able to be the way they were before it occurred. That's impossible. Life is going to be different; but there is a quality of life to be had afterwards, and this is obviously what you're trying to encourage. It may take some time, but there will be a quality of life.'

It is obvious that the talking and listening are major factors in the rehabilitation of many victims of crime. But what, I wondered, was the 'success rate'.

'I think,' she replied, 'that a very common experience of Victim Support is when we're leaving the home of a victim, and he says to us, "You have no idea what it has meant that you have come here and listened, and I'd like to thank you very much for that". I think that's the measure of our success, and, if it is, then the success rate would be about 75%. It's not 100%, but then we're not intruding into that person's life. I used to describe it in the training we did as being given the opportunity to tiptoe into someone's life for the briefest period of time; and in the time that we are there we must deal with everything we hear in the most delicate manner, so that, at the end of this time, the person would simply remember that he was feeling better, and not remember us – so that we didn't get in the way of the healing that was to take place.'

This was the kind of work in which Mollie and her helpers were busily engaged when there came that fateful day in Dunblane in March 1996.

'I was here in the house,' Mollie recalls, 'and I overheard it on the news, and I thought I'd misheard. I went through to the kitchen and put on the radio; it had just happened. So I phoned Edinburgh and then went into the office, and it was really dreadful; we were having people coming off the street into the place, because they were finding it hard to deal with the knowledge of what had happened. These were members of the public here in the town, and they were so shocked by what had happened that they wanted to express how they themselves were feeling. We also had several people, who had in some way been helped by Victim Support, phoning us, or coming in to say how sorry they were, and we spent a great deal of time listening on the telephone and in visiting people who wanted to talk about it and express their hurt at what had happened.'

Clearly, Victim Support was going to be deeply involved, and arrangements had to be put in hand to cope. Volunteer Victim Support workers were drafted in from all over Scotland, and experts on trauma came and briefed the workers about what to expect. In the event, it looked for a time as though Victim Support would be bypassed. Counselling of children was handled through Social Services and the Education Department, and the police liaised in other cases directly with Social Services. But Victim Support began to discover that people from Dunblane were beginning to contact them privately. Then an issue arose regarding application for compensation from the Criminal Injuries Compensation Board. At the time, the Board was engaged in changing its way of assessing applicants from assessment by a panel to a points-based assessment system.

This made it advisable that applications be handed in as soon as possible – in the immediate aftermath of the most violent trauma imaginable! Victim Support therefore put it out through the media that they were available to help with applications, which had the crucial side-effect of making people aware of their existence. An extra phone-line was put in, and new people began to contact them on their own initiative, without police referral. The office was inundated with calls. Many members of the children's extended families were very badly upset. Grannies and grandads were helped, uncles and aunts, family members who had put themselves 'on hold' so that they might be able to care for the mums and dads of the children, but were now feeling barely able to cope themselves.

The traumatization extended beyond the families, of course. Doctors – interestingly – did not seem to need help, but many hospital staff did, along with ambulance drivers, police and firemen. 'It was a cross-section from the whole community, really,' recalls Mollie. 'Just about every category came. You can't know what kind of person is going to be affected. For example, you don't think about the effect it is going to have on the nursing staff. I was up at the hospital when the bairns were being brought out in coffins from the mortuary. It was so sad to see a little coffin coming out in the hearse, and to know that all the hopes of the family were in that coffin. Townspeople of Dunblane were traumatized as well, because they had people from all over the world moving in; you couldn't even get accommodation in a hotel. That was an example of how bad the influx of people was at the time. Everyone was being asked to talk; everybody was expected to have a point of view. Yet this was babies you were talking about, who were members of families, of extended families, of groups of friends, who needed to be together on their own, to try to cope, with the aid of the help that was offered. At every turn there were cameras rolling, and the roads into Dunblane were blocked with traffic. People wanted to be near the place where it had happened, and of course the flowers started to accumulate at the school gate; there was a constant stream of people quite legitimately wanting to express their sympathy to the families of the victims.'

This may be the time to digress and speculate about how the surviving children at the primary school have fared. One can, and should, do no more than speculate, because to try to go further and investigate, intrude into their private trauma and grief, would be inexcusable. A clue to what kinds of things the children of Dunblane Primary School might have gone through, and may still be going through, is provided by the aftermath of an American shooting incident of some seven years earlier. Sadly, one does not have to go back to King Herod's Massacre of the Innocents to find anything comparable to Dunblane, for on 17 February 1989 a gunman called Patrick Purdy appeared at Cleveland Elementary School in Stockton, California – a school where he himself had been a pupil – and raked the children at play with gunfire. The police arrived to find five children dying, and twenty-nine wounded, as well as the body of the gunman, who had shot himself. Daniel Goleman writes in his best-selling book, *Emotional Intelligence,* of the aftermath:

'The deepest scars at Cleveland Elementary were not to the building but to the psyches of the children and staff there, who were trying to carry on with life as usual. Perhaps most striking was how the memory of those few minutes was revived again and again by any small detail that was similar in the least. A teacher told me, for example, that a wave of fright swept through the school with the announcement that St Patrick's Day was coming: a number of children somehow got the idea that the day was to honour the killer, Patrick Purdy.

'"Whenever we hear an ambulance on its way to the rest home down the street, everything halts," a teacher told me. "The kids all listen to see whether it will stop here or go on." For several weeks many children were terrified of the mirrors in the restrooms; a rumour swept the school that "Bloody Virginia Mary", some kind of fantastical monster, lurked there. Weeks after the shooting, a frantic girl came running up to the school's principal, Pat Bucher, yelling, "I hear shots! I hear shots!" The sound came from a swinging chain on a tetherball pole.

'Many children became hypervigilant, as though continually on guard against a repetition of the terror; some boys and girls would hover at recess next to the classroom doors, not daring to venture out to the playground where the killings had occurred. Others would only play in small groups, posting a designated child as lookout. They continued for months to avoid the "evil" areas, where the children had died.

'The memories lived on, too, as disturbing dreams, intruding into the children's unguarded minds as they slept. Apart from nightmares repeating the shooting itself in some way, children were flooded with anxiety dreams that left them apprehensive that they too would die soon. Some children tried to sleep with their eyes open so that they wouldn't dream.

'All of these reactions are well known to psychiatrists as among the key symptoms of post-traumatic stress disorder, or PTSD.'

Although this account comes from another time,

another place and another culture, it is valuable to us in that it gives an idea of the kinds of things that the surviving children of Dunblane have suffered and are still suffering. 'The thing is,' says Mollie, 'it's a hurt that is very much still here, and it's likely to go on for many years to come.'

Moving back into calmer waters, I asked Mollie if being a Christian made a difference to her work.

'I couldn't have become involved with Victim Support,' she answered, 'if I hadn't been a Christian. There's a huge percentage of volunteers in Victim Support who are Christians, and that would be the norm in most voluntary organizations. But there are also numbers of people who have no faith whatsoever, and they're doing a fantastic job.

'I think that, as a Christian, what helps most is the knowledge that you're never on your own, and that, as you go into each situation, you're acknowledging that the Lord is vitally concerned with the person whom you've just met, and you're quietly praying for the victim all the time you're with him. So it's very much a shared responsibility for that person. In the event of hearing something quite awful, you are able to come before the Lord to share what it is meaning to you at that particular moment in time.

'Loads of times I'm asked by other members of Victim Support staff, "How on Earth do you manage to carry on? You never seem to get overburdened like the rest of people," and I witness to them at that point.'

This is not to say that there were not times when Mollie came away from a situation feeling 'oppressed', as if there were a black cloud enveloping her. On one occasion, Sam was driving her home from a particularly terrible encounter, and the black cloud was in place. They were about to pass the gates of King's Park in

Stirling, and just inside the gate were park benches.
'Just leave me here, Sam,' said Mollie. 'I'll be all right.
Just leave me here.' She sat and looked out at the hills
and handed the threatening challenge over to God to
deal with. Gradually, she became aware of God's care
for her, and came away knowing that she would be
taken care of. Hearing the story, I am reminded of the
words of Psalm 121:1:

'I will lift up mine eyes unto the hills,
from whence cometh my help.
My help cometh from the Lord,
which made heaven and earth.'

I concluded by asking Mollie what advice she would
give to someone who had been the victim of violence,
and this was her reply:

'I would say, "Yes, what has happened to you is bad.
It shouldn't have happened, but it has happened; and
there are ways of coping and there are ways of moving
on. But as a Christian I would say that it is easier if you
are able to share that problem with others, and with
God." '

Afterword

'Why?'

After violence has happened to us, or to a loved one, this is often the word we utter, whether we are numb with shock at the time it happens, or when reflecting on it, perhaps with bitterness, a long time afterwards.

Why there is violence in the world is not a question a Christian cannot answer. The Christian faith takes as its starting point the fact that we live in a 'fallen world'; a world that is not as God intended it to be, but which has gone wrong because human beings turned against God. Genesis, the first book in the Bible, tells the story of the Fall. The story of how Adam and Eve, innocent and unashamed in their earthly paradise, chose to follow the serpent's (the devil's) advice in eating forbidden fruit. From then on, evil and suffering entered the world. The chapters that follow introduce us to Adam and Eve's descendants, who began to do evil. One of these was Lamech, the father of violence.

'Lamech said to his wives: "Adah and Zillah, listen to me. Wives of Lamech hear my words: I have killed a man for wounding me, a young man for injuring me. If Cain is avenged seven times, then Lamech is avenged seventy-seven times.' (Genesis 4:23.)

Violence is there because people have turned against God, and the stewards of creation have become its destroyers.

This does not mean that when a society like ours displays an increasing tendency towards violence no further questions need be asked. It was a fallen world fifty years ago just as it is today, and yet numbers of recorded crimes of violence in Britain were only a fraction of what they are now. There are serious questions which our society must ask itself about why violence has increased on the scale which we noted in the Introduction. Sadly, we have not got the space to begin to ask those questions here.

But the question 'Why?' is asked in another form, too, namely: 'Why did this awful thing happen to me, or to my loved one?' If one is a Christian, that question may very well take a different form, namely: 'Why did God not protect me? Why did He let it happen?' Only a few weeks before my own mugging, at the send-off from our previous church, the wives' group sang us a song based on Psalm 91:

'He will cover you with his feathers,
and under his wings you will find refuge;
His faithfulness will be your shield and rampart.'

Faced with the apparent contradiction between such promises in the Bible and the reality, Christians often fall back into a kind of atheism: atheism in practice if not in theory. They treat all that happens to them as chance, as random. If you don't take care of yourself and the things and people God has entrusted to you, they think, God will not. In fact, even if you don't take care of them because you cannot, God still will not help you. He may perhaps give you strength to cope within yourself, but in no way is He going to order events, answer prayers, intervene in the affairs of the world, bring good out of evil, or whatever.

There is a grain of truth in this attitude. Jesus taught us that the sun shines on the righteous and on the unrighteous, and the rain falls on the just and on the unjust (Matthew 5:45). If being a Christian meant that you were shielded from all that was unpleasant, and gathered up into a downy, twee, candy-floss kind of world where nothing would ever harm you again, then people (always assuming they liked the idea of such a world!) would serve God for all the wrong, selfish reasons. Likewise, they would never learn trust and compassion, or gain the character that is forged in adversity.

Some truth there may be in this stance, but it's much less than half the truth. It is an important part of our belief to affirm that 'God takes care of us'. I for one could not go on if I did not think that. The day-to-day business of living is hard enough, and often dangerous enough, for people in general; and for believers, whose faith will inevitably lead them into hardships and dangers over and above that, the Christian life would be beyond coping with if we did not truly believe that events which happen to a believer are not simply random, but have the loving hand of God in them. The promises of God in Paul's epistles (and I do find it helps enormously to accept them as just that: promises of God) give us a sharper, clearer image of what God's providence will mean. ('Providence' being the theological word for all that we are talking about.) The two promises are, firstly, I Corinthians 10:13:

'No temptation has seized you except what is common to man. And God is faithful; he will not let you be tempted beyond what you can bear. But when you are tempted, he will also provide a way out so that you can stand up under it.'

Secondly, Romans 8:28:
'And we know that in all things God works for the good of those who love him, who have been called according to his purpose.'

The first of these two promises indicates that God will not let things happen to us which destroy us as people, which we cannot bear, which will simply break us. Life may be tough, but we shall be able to cope, triumphantly. The second tells us, at any rate by implication, that God will bring good out of all things for believers, 'all things' implying things both good and bad. Will He do this for those who do not believe in Him? Perhaps He may: He loves everybody, after all. We do, however, know for certain that He will do this for believers. It's a promise.

Many of the experiences described in this book illustrate the fulfilment of these promises in our contributors' lives. And yet they do not all tell stories like these. There are some questions unanswered; and this, of course, is true of our experience in general. Some years ago a brother minister, whom I had known from college days, was caught up in serious rioting and violence in the prison where he was a chaplain. A year or so after the event, I had him over to take special services at my church, and also went with him to visit our own local prison. He was as I had always remembered him: full of energy, insights, plans, dynamism. Then, when I came to put this book together, I wrote to him, asking him if he would be willing to contribute a piece to the book concerning his experiences at the time of the prison riots. I got a short letter back saying that he and his doctors felt that it would not be helpful to him to contribute, because he had been invalided out of the ministry with post-traumatic stress disorder. The reply was haunting, not only because it illustrated how the psychological consequences of violence can have a delayed onset – years, in his case – but because one cannot help but wonder why. What was God doing, allowing a gifted minister to fall by the wayside at a comparatively early age?

There is no short answer to that question, either in his case or in any other case that raises the same issue. Perhaps we should not try too hard to answer the question for people involved in such situations, for if we do we tend to become glib and false. It is better just to wait.

Later on in the book of Genesis (from chapter 37), there is the story of Jacob's son Joseph, and his ten brothers. Joseph was the youngest but one, the ablest, and unfortunately the cockiest of his family. He had dreams which his brothers rightly interpreted as mean-ing he would rule over them. And he was his father's undisguised favourite, as his 'coat of many colours', made for him by his father, only too clearly indicated. His jealous brothers set upon him and did him vio-lence, throwing him into a pit in the desert, whence he was 'rescued' and sold to Midianite slave traders.

In slavery in Egypt, Joseph did very well, until his master's wife attempted unsuccessfully to seduce him and maliciously had him thrown into prison.

The story goes on to relate how Joseph gained a rep-utation in gaol as an interpreter of dreams, which led to his being asked to interpret Pharaoh's dreams and then to have oversight of Pharaoh's affairs. The saga of

Joseph – one of the longest continuous stories in the Bible – ends with his brothers coming to seek corn in Egypt in a time of famine, for which the Egyptians had stored up corn in readiness at Joseph's advice, and eventually, after a process of softening up, to their reconciliation with him.

God had been at work in the situation to provide for their need and bring about reconciliation. 'God meant it for good,' says Joseph to his brothers. But if someone had asked Joseph where God was during the years he spent in prison, and what God was doing in his life at that time, he might have been at a loss for an answer. So, too, in some stories of violence: we don't know what God is doing now, but we shall hereafter.

God's promises remain true all the same. He is a faithful God who will not let us down. We must, however, remember that He often works by using difficulty and pain to bring about good. We are not exempted from trouble and suffering and it would not be right if we were, but the difference for the believer is that God takes up the things that should not have happened, that were not what He wanted, and weaves them into the fabric of His will. In so doing, He gives to these events, traumatic though they were, a meaning. In the process of healing, it is of some value for the victim and his loved ones to recognize the event as having some meaning and value.

I once knew a Vietnam veteran, now working as a businessman in the United Kingdom, who went through the hell of that tragic war. Then, as he stepped off the plane onto American soil, a young woman approached him. 'I thought,' he said, 'that she was going to embrace me, or put flowers round my neck, or something. But she didn't. She spat in my face.' It must have made the healing process for him, and for other returned soldiers, all the more difficult as what they had been through was not valued. If there had been medals and cheering and embraces, it would have endowed their ordeal with value, and helped the healing process.

There are also the 'How?' questions. How do I adjust? How do I go on living a decent quality of life? How do I find peace of mind again? How is healing to be found?

Make no mistake: when someone is recovering from violence, the most serious wounds are the ones which cannot be seen, the wounds to the mind and heart. Healing is needed. Nowadays there is even a name to put to the disorder.

In 1980, the American Psychiatric Association brought out the third edition of its 'bible', *The Diagnostic and Statistical Manual of Mental Disorders*. In it, along with all the other forms of mental illness (which had been understood for perhaps centuries in some cases), there was a new category of disorder listed, namely 'Post Traumatic Stress Disorder'. This was not an unknown illness; the 'Shell-Shock' of World War I was surely the same thing by another name; but this was the first time that its origins and symptoms had been clarified and set down. Interestingly enough – and here, perhaps, is another example of God's bringing good out of evil – it was through research carried out on Vietnam war veterans during the 1970s that the nature of the illness was clarified. The sufferer typically will experience things like depression, poor sleep, nightmares, a permanent hyper-vigilance, an edginess and a tendency to be easily startled; and most characteristic of all, 'flashbacks', which are not so much vivid memories of traumatic events as a reliving of them, as if they are happening to the victim all over again.

Typically, the sound of a car backfiring, say, might trigger off in the sufferer a reliving of the occasion when his buddy, walking along beside him, was shot and received dreadful, fatal injuries. He will feel again all that he felt then.

Research has established that severe trauma can result in an alteration of the brain structure, whereby certain chemical substances which the brain produces in times of emergency continue to be produced too readily and in too great quantities. These substances include the 'catecholamines' adrenaline and noradrenalin, the hormone CRF, and endorphins, which blunt the feeling of pain. These are responsible for the distressing symptoms. Other research done at that time into the same disorder throws an interesting light on why one person experiencing an act of violence of a certain severity will suffer PTSD badly, while another experiencing violence of equal severity will not suffer it at all. The clue lies in the degree of helplessness experienced by the victim. If he knew, being perhaps a policeman, that he was likely to be approached by someone armed with a knife, and knew how to cope either verbally or physically with the knifeman, then even though he did in the end receive a wound, this mental trauma would be nothing like as severe as that of a victim who wasn't expecting the attack, who didn't know at all how to cope with it when it came, and who thought he would be killed.

This knowledge is invaluable to us, especially those of us who have to live out the Gospel among tough and unhappy characters, because it shows us that if we can pick up hints about how to talk to and deal with the violent person, and if we learn how to seek the 'peace that passes understanding' within ourselves, then not only are we going to be better equipped to defuse violent situations, but, also, if we are still attacked, we shall be less traumatized because we'll feel less helpless. Christ's peace can be cultivated, and the instructions as to how to do so are clearly given in the New Testament in Philippians 4:4-7:

'Rejoice in the Lord always. I will say it again: Rejoice! Let your gentleness be evident to all. The Lord is near. Do not be anxious about anything, but in everything, by prayer and petition, with thanksgiving, present your requests to God. And the peace of God, which transcends all understanding, will guard your hearts and your minds in Christ Jesus.'

To what extent is PTSD curable? This obviously will depend to a degree on how severe it is, and what Mollie has to say in the chapter about her work suggests that it will depend also on how loving and supportive and positive the environment is in which the victim finds himself; but medically speaking we say it can be remedied, though not without some residual problems. The way to healing lies through gradually recalling memories of the event in an environment of security, say, with a trusted therapist. The memories may come gradually and should be allowed to do so, but the more detailed and full and vivid they are when spoken out, the more complete will be the healing. It is as if the victim is gradually taking over control of the memories, rather than their having control of him, and his brain is, in addition, learning a useful lesson, that loving security may be experienced in tandem with the memories of trauma. The Christian can learn from this the importance of both being a listener and being listened to.

When the founder of the Clinical Theology Movement, Dr Frank Lake, brought out his 600-page text-book on Clinical Theology, he opened his treatment with a one-hundred-page chapter devoted simply to the 'Ministry of Listening'. One is reminded of how, in the book of Job, Job – himself a victim of violence along with his other misfortunes – rounds on his talkative, canting, insensitive friends with all their standard pieties, and says, 'Listen to what I am saying; that is all the comfort I ask from you.' (Job 21:1, 2, GNB.) Some of our stories reveal a serious failure on the part of Christians to understand this need.

For a Christian, there are other dimensions to the process of healing the victim of trauma. It is most help-ful if the victim can be prayed *with*, and not merely prayed *for*. Remember how helpful 'M' found this to be. The process of prayer should also involve *listening* to God, rather than merely beseeching Him for help. Developments in the last thirty years of Church history have brought home to us the value of receiving words and insights from God. Time and again these are found to unlock the cause of a sufferer's pain, and this will be an indication of how one should pray for him, or an invitation to the victim to open up.

On one occasion known to me, one troubled woman was being prayed for by a friend and a picture of a child's shoe floated into the friend's mind. She shared this with the woman, who promptly broke down in tears. She had been mistreated by her mother as a child, and had on one traumatic occasion been physi-cally abused because she had put her tiny shoe down the toilet. Thus the area of hurt was opened up. Such a ministry may be the way forward for many, if conduc-ted by wise, mature Christians.

So victims of violence need not be robbed of their peace of mind permanently. All the contributors to this

book are lively, caring, vibrant people, despite all
they've been through. Perhaps even because of it. We
should put nothing beyond God's power to heal. Time
alone, however, does not necessarily heal. There is a
need to share our troubles with those who will listen
and those who will pray.

There remain a number of vexed questions to answer.

Most pressing is the problem of domestic violence,
which, of course, raises a whole range of additional
issues. Joanne's case illustrates so clearly the kind of
problems faced by a Christian woman who finds herself
caught up in a violent marriage, and hauntingly
reminds us that violence can occur even in a marriage
where both parties are devout Christians. Joanne's
experience, and those of other women victims whose
stories are told in these pages, shows how individual
Christians, and the Christian Church, badly need to
learn some 'new tricks' in coping with such problems.
The battered wife and her helpers need to be very clear
about a number of points:

Firstly, it is not her fault, and would only ever
become her fault if the husband had experienced
repeated violence from *her*, and had snapped finally, or
was defending himself. Nothing justifies violence
between marriage partners. Malachi 2:16 may say, ' "I
hate divorce," says the Lord God of Israel,' but it then
goes on immediately, ' "and I hate a man's covering
himself with violence as well as with his garment." '
Violence against one's marriage partner has no place in
the Christian – or any other – life.

Secondly, blaming oneself, being subservient and
hoping that one's husband will have a change of heart,
does not work. Accepting blame, promising to be better,
and covering the wounds up, merely allows the batter-
er to continue deceiving himself that he is not blame-

worthy. Tough though it is, it is a more loving thing to confront him with the misery he is causing. It may be right for his minister (if the husband is a Christian) to have a talk with him, but it needs to be appreciated that, in such circumstances, the husband might well receive the minister kindly and then afterwards administer a particularly severe beating to his wife for telling on him. The best advice is to get out of the situation altogether.

Thirdly, where there are children, the wife *must* get the children out of the situation. They need not actually be victims of battering themselves to be lastingly damaged by it. They only need to be aware that it goes on. Many wife batterers were themselves brought up in circumstances of domestic violence. Just as it is wrong to put 'a stumbling-block in the way of one of those little ones' (to use our Lord's language in Mark 9:42), so it is wrong to expose children to an atmosphere of violence.

Another question concerns the use of force on the part of the one attacked. When *should* one use force? I think the clearest answer is, when the object is to prevent violence being done to a third party, when all else has failed and force is unlikely to make matters worse for him. When force is used, it should be the minimum necessary to defend the victim against the attack.

For oneself, however, when one only has oneself to defend, there are two possibilities. ● One is to take what Jesus says in Matthew chapter 5 about 'turning the other cheek' as a prohibition of all violence, and opt to defend oneself only by talking, or not to defend oneself at all. ● The other is to take it as a prohibition of *revenge*, which is not the same as the use of force in self-defence or the defence of others at the point when it is needed; in which case a Christian is free to defend himself or herself with minimum force.

I am inclined towards the second option. It is particularly hard to suggest to a victim of rape, especially, that she should allow her attacker to carry on without resistance. It has to be said, however, that in most of the stories told in this book, use of force by the victim would have been highly dangerous or impossible: there must be many cases where the question of self-defence simply does not arise.

And then there is the question of forgiveness. Ought we to forgive our attacker? Yes. It is a hard reply, but yes, we must, totally and completely. It is a particularly hard answer to give, not to the victim, but to those who love the victim. The victim's loved ones almost always find it harder to forgive than the victim does. Yet forgive we must. *This is not, however, the same thing as refusing to press charges against one's attacker.* We may bear him no ill will, but it would be wrong to allow him to continue roaming free to wreak violence against other people.

There are two reasons for forgiving. One is that it is commanded by Jesus (Matthew 5:43, 44; 18:21, 22, and in many other verses). The other is that long-standing bitterness is profoundly unhealthy, having a seriously destructive effect on the wronged person's happiness, his peace of mind, and his relationship with God. Bitterness is a nasty little room, the door of which is marked 'forgiveness'. That door doesn't open easily, and you may have to shove it open again and again, day by day, for a while until it stays open, but it is the way out. *Leave the revenge to God.*

In conclusion, I would remind the reader that to be a victim of violence, though it is one of life's nastiest experiences, is not the end of joy or of hope. Healing will sometimes come with time. More often it needs some help. That help is to be found in 'sharing it with others, and with God'.